CLASSICAL ATTITUDES
TO MODERN ISSUES

Classical Attitudes to Modern Issues

L. P. WILKINSON

Population and Family Planning
Women's Liberation
Nudism in Deed and Word
Homosexuality

WILLIAM KIMBER · LONDON

Published in 1979 by
WILLIAM KIMBER & CO. LIMITED
Godolphin House, 22a Queen Anne's Gate
London SW1H 9AE

© L. P. Wilkinson, 1978

ISBN 0 7183 0326 1

MADE AND PRINTED IN GREAT BRITAIN BY
THE GARDEN CITY PRESS LIMITED
LETCHWORTH, HERTFORDSHIRE
SG6 1JS

For
Duncan Taylor

Contents

NOTE ON THE DUSTCOVER

Aristogiton and Harmodius (see page 115) were lovers, elder and younger respectively. Erotic advances were made to Harmodius by Hipparchus, younger brother of Hippias the tyrant of Athens, so the lovers planned to kill them both (514 BC). The plot miscarried, and Hipparchus alone was killed. Harmodius was cut down by bodyguards, and Aristogiton arrested, tortured and executed. Three years later the tyranny was overthrown, and thereafter the lovers, whose act was seen as the spark that ignited the train leading to the revolution, were idealised by the Athenian democracy. Their descendants were granted for ever the right to dine free in the Prytaneum hall. Statues of them carried off by Xerxes in 480 were replaced in 477 by a pair from the hands of Critius and Nesiotes, showing them a moment after the killing of Hipparchus, which stood in the Agora. Our dustcover is from a good copy in the Museo Nazionale at Naples.

It is pertinent to one *raison d'être* of the present book to add, by way of example, that even the 1970 edition of the *Oxford Classical Dictionary* devotes more than two hundred words to the story (*s.v.* 'Aristogiton') without mentioning that the two were lovers or that their 'private differences' with the tyrants were of erotic origin.

Introduction

WHEN I received the flattering invitation to give
the Lord Northcliffe Memorial Lectures at University
College London I cast about for a subject
within my field, the classics, which might be of interest
to an audience which would probably be drawn from
other fields besides. My own work had been largely
concerned with those virtues of Latin literature which
depend on the Latin language, besides presupposing a
fairly detailed familiarity with Greek and Roman literary
history. Even my special interest in classical influences
on later literature might be too specialised; and in
any case I doubted whether I could find enough that
was both unfamiliar and worth saying on that subject
to fill four lectures. It then occurred to me that there
were topics of particular interest in these days of social
revolution to which the ideas and experience of the
ancient Greeks and Romans were highly relevant.
Moreover, there were aspects of these topics which, so
far as my knowledge went, had not been sufficiently
aired in writing and conversation about the classics
even among specialists, let alone in popular hand-

books, because until the last two or three decades they had been taboo.[1] Indeed, I was all too hazy about some of these matters myself when I began my investigations.

I hope that no one would dispute that the four topics I have chosen are of prime interest at the present time. As to population, a great deal of work has been devoted to trying to estimate the size of ancient populations, less perhaps to what the ancients themselves thought about it; and as to its corollary, family planning, too little has been said in popularising works about infanticide, for instance, partly perhaps because of a vestigial reluctance to believe ill of the idealised Greeks, and too little about abortion and contraceptive methods, discussion of which has only recently freed itself from traditional secretiveness. Yet the ideas of one of the most intelligent societies that have ever existed on issues so vital to us cannot fail to be highly relevant.

On women's liberation more has been said, but incidentally no general disquisition on woman's place in antiquity. Here the relevance is largely one of contrast, but not entirely; and for once the Romans were in some ways more civilised that the Greeks. Nudism indeed, with its unique place in Greek athletics and all that radiated from that, has not, I think, been sufficiently discussed as a social phenomenon, and nudism in word in antiquity still less. And finally, homosexuality has been too often skated over, or treated in the light, or rather the shadow, of agelong prejudices that have

[1] Illustrated books on art have also too often drawn a veil. Thus in the 21 sections in W. Zschietzschmann's *Hellas and Rome: the Classical World in Pictures* (1959) there is none on sexual relationships, though they figured prominently in art.

only begun to dissolve in the past two or three decades.

The four lectures were delivered at University College London, most generous and considerate of hosts, on January 12, 15, 19 and 22, 1976, under the general title of 'Classical Approaches to Modern Topics'. For various reasons they did not reach print until the numbers of *Encounter* for April, May, August and September, 1978, where the titles on the covers and the illustrations were chosen by the magazine. No attempt was made to rewrite them either then or for this collected edition, which owes its existence to the initiative of Mr William Kimber: they are in all essentials as delivered at the beginning of 1976.

The secondary sources I consulted, let alone the primary ones, were very numerous and variegated, and I am deeply conscious of my debt to the writers. I will mention here only two or three writings that I was fortunate enough to be able to read in time which stand out in my mind as particularly illuminating discussions of an aspect. The first is an article by K. J. (Sir Kenneth) Dover on Greek attitudes to homosexuality entitled 'Eros and Nomos' (*Bulletin of the London University Institute of Classical Studies*, 1964). The second is the unpublished dissertation entitled 'The later Roman Aristocracy: a demographic profile' by my former pupil M. Keith Hopkins, now Professor of Sociology at Brunel University, which won him his Fellowship of King's College, Cambridge, in 1963, and an article that sprang from it, 'Contraception in the Roman Empire' (*Comparative Studies in Society and History* VIII, 1965–6, 124–51).

I am grateful to my friends Mr Donald Lucas, Dr Geoffrey Lloyd and Dr Anthony Bulloch for reading the original typescript of the lectures, and to Professor Meyer Fortes, Canon G. B. Bentley, Dr C. B. Goodhart and Dr J. G. Keogh of York University, Toronto, for suggestions made following the *Encounter* publication. And finally, I must thank the then Provost of University College London, Lord Annan, and its Lord Northcliffe Lectureship Committee for inviting me to give the lectures; the editors of *Encounter* for first printing them; and now William Kimber & Company for giving them this more permanent existence.

PATRICK WILKINSON

September 1978

ONE

I

Population and Family Planning

IN this chapter, when I speak of population I shall
not be concerned with the vexed question of figures,
and the extent to which they can be deduced for antiquity, but only with Greek and Roman attitudes to the
subject, which did sometimes affect political theory,
practical policy, and private family planning.

The spectre of global overpopulation does not seem
to have been in the forefront of men's minds until quite
recently. Of course anxiety about population in general terms was sparked off by Malthus' essay of 1798;
and it haunts such books as J. S. Mill's *Principles of
Political Economy* (1848). But people were mainly concerned about the particular society to which they
belonged. I was therefore surprised to find John
Addington Symonds writing in 1891 of 'our age when
the habitable portions of the globe are rapidly becoming overcrowded . . .'. The expansion has notoriously
become an explosion since the wholesale export to
underdeveloped countries of the benefits of Western
progress in medicine and hygiene, through the agency
of the international health organisations that came into

15

being with the League of Nations and its successor the United Nations. The concomitant acceptance by the more prosperous nations of at least some measure of responsibility for feeding the famished millions has increased awareness that we are 'One World'. Yet I think F. L. Lucas was justified when he wrote, only some sixteen years ago, of what he called 'The Greatest Problem of Today' as being 'chastely avoided by the popular press'. Pope Paul VI, addressing the United Nations as lately as 1965, gave as his message: 'Your task is so to labour that bread will be sufficiently abundant at the table of humanity, and not unreasonably[1] to favour an artificial control of birth in order to reduce the number of guests at the banquet of life.' But is it only a matter of bread? It was calculated not long ago that, if the present increase in proliferation were unchecked, there would be in 600 years' time very little standing room for each human being. Yet even the alarming, some would say, alarmist, manifesto issued by a group of scientists in 1972 entitled 'A Blueprint for Survival' seems to have created little more than a temporary stir.

In antiquity there is one very early reference to global overpopulation. It occurs in the exordium salvaged from the lost sixth (or seventh) century epic called the *Cypria*, which was composed to cover the Tale of Troy up to the events described in the *Iliad*. The *Iliad* opens with a description of the slaughter caused by the wrath

---

[1] 'Unreasonably', in this official translation, might suggest that artificial control of birth is all right 'within reason'. The original French text reads, *'un contrôle artificiel des naissances, qui serait irrationnel'. Acta Apostolica*, 1965.

of Achilles and adds parenthetically: 'It was the will of Zeus that was being fulfilled'. By the time the *Cypria* was composed men had begun to demand that gods should not be less moral than mortals. So to justify the ways of Homer's Zeus to men the author attributed to him the motive of pity: he stirred up the Trojan War to relieve the world of overpopulation. This fantastic idea obtained sufficient currency in literary tradition to be twice echoed by Euripides. More importantly, enlarged to include all causes of mass death, it figured in the theodicy of the Stoic Chrysippus. And from the providential Zeus of the Stoics it was transferred to the Christian God by Tertullian, with more immediate reference to an existing situation. Writing about AD 200 in North Africa, a province with an exceptional and expanding amount of population, he said:

> Our numbers are burdensome to the world, which can hardly supply us from its natural elements. . . . Pestilence, famine, war and earthquakes should be regarded as a remedy for the nations, a means of pruning the luxuriance of the human race.

But both in ancient and in modern times discussion of population has primarily been in terms of individual states. The nation-states of modern Europe assumed for centuries that an increase in population was a good thing, simply for the sake of competitive power. Machiavelli urged the idea, and the French legislation of Colbert in 1664 embodied it; and there were Old Testament texts to encourage it. 'Increase and multiply and replenish the earth.' In our own times Mussolini and Hitler awarded prizes for large families; and the Japanese war-lords in 1939 banned birth-control, aiming to have a population of 100,000,000 by 1960. I say nothing of General de Gaulle. But these were by now aberrations. What sober people have become concerned about is the *optimum* population for their country, and whether there should be a government policy about it. In 'A Blueprint for Survival' the optimum population for Britain was estimated to be 30,000,000. Discussion in terms of economics, agriculture and imports of food has been overtaken by discussion about the environment and the quality of life. Thus highrise buildings originated in anxiety about the supply of development land: now we worry about their psychological effect. The Conservation Society debates whether its main concern is birth-control or amenities; in the long run the latter may depend on the former.

In Ancient Greece the problem arose as soon as the more settled conditions of the eighth century BC permitted population to grow in a Malthusian way. The small, mountain-locked states soon became unable to support themselves. At first colonisation provided an outlet. This continued until the sixth century, after which there was opposition in the West from the Carthaginians, Etruscans, and Illyrians; and the suitable sites around the Aegean Sea were all occupied. Cities then began to grow, and to produce goods, with the help of captured slaves, partly in order to pay by exports for the corn they now had to import.

This was especially so in Athens, the state about which we know most. In the fifty years following the Persian Wars she paid for corn for her growing population by the export of oil and the pottery that held it, though even more by the tribute of her empire and by the silver from her mines at Laurium. But the slaves themselves had to be fed; she lost her empire in the Peloponnesian War; and the silver mines gave out. In 346 we find the Athenian publicist Isocrates appealing to Philip of Macedon to lead a pan-Hellenic crusade of conquest against Persia, so as not only to unite Greece, but also to provide an outlet for her surplus population, which had turned to banditry. The conquests of Philip's son Alexander the Great were to implement his policy for a while.

In these circumstances people had begun to think about *optimum* population for their states, towards the end of the colonising period. We hear that Phidon of Corinth aimed at keeping the number of families and of citizens static, while Philolaus laid down for Thebes laws about procreation intended to keep the number of lots of land the same. It is unfortunate that we do not know what measures they adopted. When theorists began to devise ideal states, they addressed themselves to the problem with an eye to the quality of life for a leisured class. Plato in his *Republic*, having abolished marriage at least for his élite of guardians, provided that sexual intercourse among them should be regulated by the rulers in such a way as to keep the population stable, taking account of probable losses through war, disease, etc. [2]

[2] At II 372 Plato says that citizens must not beget offspring beyond their means, lest they fall into poverty or war. But he seems to accept it as inevitable that, with the expected rise in the standard of living, there will be predatory conquests which will require a professional army both for aggression and defence. It is in this context, indeed, that his 'guardians' are first mentioned (II 374).

In the less revolutionary utopian work of his old age, the *Laws*, he restored the institution of marriage; but the rearing of families was still to be governed by the interests of the state. He fixed on 5,040 as a suitable number of plot-holders (perhaps as a number which conveniently happened to be divisible by every factor from 2 to 12 except 11). For stability's sake this number must remain the same for ever. Each plot-holder must leave a single male heir, surrendering any further sons for adoption by the sonless, and marrying off his daughters. (Plato omits to make any provision about family planning for the subservient classes. As regards the number of plot-holders they were irrelevant; but as mouths to feed they certainly were not.)

Aristotle, in his critique of Plato's *Laws*, considers 5,040 plot-holders far too many, in view of the women and retainers who must be added. He also considers Plato far too sanguine in assuming here that population will be kept stable by an automatic balance between sterile and overfertile marriages, a problem that would not have arisen in his marriage-less *Republic*. In fact, Aristotle says, failure to control the size of the population is a constant cause of poverty in states, and so of crime and rebellion. Numbers should be regulated by calculating the chances of mortality in children and of sterility in marriage (easier said than done before the age of statistics). A state should be large enough to be self-sufficient, but small enough to be easily comprehended. Here he puts his finger on what it was that made the city-state viable in human terms.

But of course states had to breed a sufficient number of soldiers; and we hear more, in troubled times, of underpopulation than of overpopulation. This was especially true of Sparta, where the 'Spartiate' élite had to hold down a much larger subject population. In the fifth century (possibly as a result of a devastating earthquake in 465 but more probably owing to a process of social erosion) she became worried about her manpower. At all events we know that at some time she introduced severe penalties for celibacy as well as rewards for child-bearing. She was seriously concerned even about the loss of the 124 Spartiates trapped by the Athenians on the island of Sphacteria in 424. By the time of her débâcle at Leuctra in 371 she had only 1,000 of these; whereas Aristotle calculated that her territory could have maintained 30,000 infantry and 1,500 cavalry. Unwillingness to breed because of a decadent obsession with personal wealth seemed to be the chief cause. Nor was there, as in Athens, a strong religious cult of ancestors to motivate perpetuation of the family.

Pericles, in his funeral oration of 430 BC in Thucydides, impressed on the bereaved parents of Athens their duty to breed more sons to replace the dead; and emergency husband-sharing is said to have been introduced for this purpose after the Sicilian disaster of 413. Nevertheless in the world of the fourth century Attic Orators families even of five children are not uncommon. It may be that, before what we call the Hellenistic Age (the two centuries following the death of Alexander in 323), only the really poor had to resort to extreme measures of family restriction. The sense of solidarity, pride, and communal purpose that characterised the independent city-state was still operative.

Aristotle was concerned only about *over*-population in a limited city-state. He gave no thought to the possibility of *under*population in larger communities. But his pupil Alexander's conquests emasculated the city-states and weakened their patriotic spirit. Perhaps for this reason there was, by the second century BC, widespread *under*population in Greece.[3] The historian Polybius deplored this. People were reluctant to marry, or at least to rear children. If they reared any, it was only one or two, who might easily die early and so extinguish the family. He ascribed this to selfishness and indolence, and to a desire to give one's children too high a standard of living. But it may equally well have been due to demoralisation and reluctance to bring children into a world of incessant war, revolution, banditry and violence in general, with a high chance of poverty, enslavement or early death. And if it is true that Aemilius Paullus, after defeating King Perseus of Macedon at Pydna in 167, carried off 150,000 into slavery from the region of Epirus alone, there we have an example of one cause of depopulation, and of demoralisation among the remnants.

The Romans were from early times an ambitious and expansive people. Their word '*proletarii*' means 'breeders'. Traditions about measures designed to increase the population that had been enacted in the

---

[3] That this continued into the time of Augustus, in spite of comparative freedom from wars and epidemics under the Pax Romana, is clear from the geographer Strabo's account of various districts. It was still true in the time of Plutarch (*c.* AD 100). Athens, however, revived under Rome, and Egypt and the Middle East were populous and prosperous.

good old days were current in the late Republic. Cicero embodied these measures in his idealising work *On the Laws*. Even if they were apocryphal, or in abeyance, the belief in them is evidence of contemporary anxiety about population. The measures mooted from the time of the Gracchi (in the late second century BC) and onwards for founding colonies overseas and settling surplus population on the land in Italy had mainly to do with the unemployed in the Capital, who had otherwise to be kept alive by corn subsidies: they do not indicate citizen overpopulation in general. On the land, slaves had been taking the place of citizens; and, in the city, the all-important upper classes were breeding less. In 131 BC the censor Metellus Macedonicus made a speech to the Senate 'On Increasing Offspring' in which he seems to have advocated making marriage compulsory. Cicero in his speech *'Pro Marcello'* urged upon the dictator Caesar the need to encourage reproduction.

Finally Augustus, who had Metellus' old speech read out in the Senate, introduced legislation penalising celibates and childless couples and giving privileges to those who had three children. In his time the problem had been aggravated by the number of deaths caused by the Civil Wars. That it was not merely the ruling class whose birth-rate Augustus wished to stimulate, is shown by his offering privileges for child-bearing even to freedwomen, though they had to produce four. The Elder Pliny tells of a freedman from Fiesole who was given the reward of processing to the Capitol with his eight children, twenty-seven grandchildren and eighteen great-grandchildren. Augustus' measures, though they provoked strong reactions and apparently remained ineffective, were still hopefully re-enacted by other emperors for three centuries.

Yet even three surviving children per family would have been insufficient to maintain the population, given the prevailing death-rate. Infant mortality in antiquity has been estimated at ten times that for England today; and adults also died on average much younger. The two Gracchi, for instance, with one sister, were the only survivors to maturity of twelve siblings. Yet even so, private birth-control must always have been a major factor in determining population. This fact has been obscured by the natural reticence which inhibits people from talking about such subjects as infanticide, abortion, and contraception, especially as regards themselves personally, an inhibition indicated by the use of euphemisms, such as the Greek *apothesis* ('disposal'), for the exposure of babies (like our phrase 'putting down' for killing pets).

As a transition to the subject of Family Planning it will be convenient here to consider eugenics. Positive eugenics, the mating of suitable persons to produce a superior breed (such as was attempted to some extent in Hitler's Nazi *SS*), were prescribed by Plato in the *Republic*. To prevent heart-burning, the selection of participants was to be disguised by a faked ballot. Both Plato and Aristotle provided in their ideal states that parents should breed only when in their prime. Plato puts this for women at from twenty to forty years of age, for men from the end of their prowess at racing until fifty (just like stud horses). Aristotle wished women to marry at eighteen, men at 37: then they were in the prime of life respectively, and the decline in the powers of both would coincide.

In Sparta, we are told, positive eugenics were put into practice. An elderly man with a young wife might introduce to her some handsome young man, and adopt the resultant offspring; or a worthy man who admired some woman for the fine children she had borne might obtain her husband's permission to beget children for himself on her. Spartans thought it illogical of other peoples to breed horses and dogs eugenically, but to keep wives jealously under one individual's lock and key. The physical training of Spartan girls was intended to enable them to produce strong boys.

Plato also proposed negative eugenics. The worst should cohabit with the worst in as few cases as possible, and their offspring should be made to disappear in some obscure unmentioned place (note the euphemisms), as should any defective offspring of superior parents. Aristotle, too, prescribed that no defective child should be reared. This was common form in antiquity. In Sparta new-born babies were brought by their parents to the elders of their tribe; and if these judged them unpromising, they were thrown into a chasm near the foot of Mount Taÿgetus. At Rome the early code of law called the Twelve Tables enjoined the suppression of abnormal babies—the very abnormal were regarded with horror as portents from the gods. Even the gentle Seneca remarks casually: 'Monstrous offspring we suppress, and we drown infants that are weakly or abnormal.' Of course, to some extent the suppression of the deformed was an act of mercy. (A doctor recently made bold to state publicly that he had on occasion, with the parents' consent, not assisted a child born with *spina bifida* to live, and recommended that this should be standard practice.)

25

But negative eugenics apart, what do we know of family planning in antiquity, and how it was attempted?

Though production of legitimate offspring was enjoined and generally accepted in theory as being a duty required for the survival of the state and for the maintenance of the rites of the dead, of whom you would some day be one yourself, the main considerations seem to have been personal. The earlier Greeks probably thought it would be nice in theory to have a large family, but quite unrealistic: there simply was not enough land to go round. Hesiod, about 700 BC, is our first witness. He recommends that a farmer should rear one son only, so that the inheritance may not be divided. He had a special reason for feeling this: his poem, the *Works and Days*, professes to be motivated by a dispute with his brother Perses over the division of their inheritance, in which he thought he had been badly treated. Presumably he would have acquiesced, as a social duty, in rearing a daughter as well; and indeed, in his vivid description of winter, he does not forget to mention the tender young girl sitting cosily at the fireside. Democritus, about 400 BC, said that while it is natural to want to beget children of your own, adoption, which allowed of choice, was more sensible. A comic poet quipped that the only thing more wretched than a man with children was a man with more children.

Poverty was, according to the historian Appian, the reason why the Roman poor in the second century BC were no longer able to rear children. But there was, as we saw, for the opposite reason, a reluctance to breed among the Roman rich as well. It began with the influx of booty and tribute in the era of conquest following the Hannibalic War. Desire to have one son and heir did persist, but less often desire to have more, in a society where the inheritance was equally shared between all sons and daughters. Inheritances were in any case much curtailed by prestige expenditure, which sumptuary laws failed to curb. Expensive games had to be put on in the name of any son desiring a political career, and daughters required dowries commensurate to their father's status.

Meanwhile, religious belief had weakened, and with it anxiety about having no children to attend to the cult of your spirit after death. In the upper strata of society (of which we hear most) marriages were arranged alliances and were not warmly regarded as means to sexual gratification. Husbands could obtain that from the nearest attractive freedwoman or slave, or from a more permanent concubine of his own choice; and any resultant children had the status of the mother and, if they were reared at all, need never be seen, much less recognised, by their father. The highly respectable Plutarch actually advises a bride to be grateful to her husband if, out of respect for her, he works off his passions on a courtesan or slave. Wives, for their part, were emancipated, and less willing, in a sexually competitive society, to risk spoiling their beauty temporarily by pregnancies or permanently by childbirth. Pregancy was in any case a burden, and childbirth a pain and a danger.

In such a social atmosphere it was no wonder families tended to be small. The normal ideal was something like Cicero's, one daughter and one son. If a son was born first, you might dispense with a daughter. It was noted that seven successive Domitii who became consul were only sons. The ultimate repudiation of the *mos maiorum* comes from Seneca of all people: 'The most fatuous thing in the world,' he says, 'is to marry and have children in order to perpetuate one's name, or to have support in old age, or to secure that you have an heir. . . .' But perhaps that was just his rhetoric.

Family planning, however, was not easy, owing to the high mortality rate in the young. If you allowed for too much wastage, you might find yourself obliged to cripple the family's fortunes by divided inheritance. It was safer to offer for adoption any surplus children you might have on your hands and rely on adopting an adult yourself if eventually you were left with no heir. But you might get caught. The case of Aemilius Paullus was famous. He gave the two sons he had by his first marriage to a Fabius and a Scipio for adoption, only to see the two sons of his second marriage die in boyhood on the eve of his crowning victory at Pydna.

But, you will have been asking yourselves, if families in long periods of antiquity were so small, how did this come about? For even allowing for the high mortality rate, and for an age of marriage for men which was late by our standards,[4] uninhibited marital relations might have been expected to produce more surviving offspring. And how was it that St Augustine, in his

----

[4] Xenophon said that, since men do not marry for sexual satisfaction, it was best not to marry before thirty, when sexual desire is less keen, to avoid having too many children. Aristotle thought that girls who married too young were inconveniently demanding as to sexual intercourse.

Manichaean period, lived twelve years with a concubine yet produced only one child, conceived in the first year?

First of all we must consider the possibility of simple self-restraint. This was what Plato expected of his guardians while they were within the breeding age—with only occasional stud performances for selected sires and dams, at specially arranged festivals ('worse than monasticism', A. E. Taylor called it). Plato regarded sexual desire as a morbid condition, to be controlled and directed to expediency, not pleasure. Self-denial in sexual matters, he said, was quite practicable: indeed it was practised by Olympic athletes in training. He anticipated Dr Thomas Arnold in prescribing exercise as an antidote, with regard to young men below the age prescribed for marriage. Sexual acts of any kind outside wedlock were to be so discouraged by social disapproval that in time they would become as much taboo as incest. Failing that, he would legislate against them. This attitude is found later among some Stoics (notably Musonius Rufus in the first century AD, who thought that all sexual activity not aimed at procreation was wrong). The Christian Lactantius said that anyone too poor to raise children must practise abstinence, not indulge in non-reproductive modes of sex. But where there was no religious sanction it is unlikely that such abstinence was widespread.

Non-reproductive modes of sex must not be overlooked as a possible form of birth-control. Aristotle mentions, but does not pursue, the possibility that the organised homosexuality of Crete may have been intended to keep down the population, and, intention apart, it may have had that effect.[5] And in heterosexual intercourse also, oral, anal and onanistic methods may have been employed. Plato condemns what he vaguely calls 'sowing the seed on stony ground where it cannot bear fruit'. This subject is rarely mentioned in classical literature, partly no doubt through a natural reticence broken only by intentionally obscene writers such as Catullus and Martial. There is an odd reference, however, in Herodotus. Pisistratus, the sixth-century Athenian ruler, not wanting for particular reasons to have children by his second wife, had intercourse with her in unorthodox ways. It is a remarkable fact that *coitus interruptus*, until recent times by far the most widely used method of birth-control in the West,[6] is not mentioned in classical literature in the thousand years that separate the poet Archilochus (if a recently discovered papyrus fragment is rightly attributed and interpreted) and St Augustine.

But we must beware of thinking that practices condemned by Christians were new. They may simply have been unmentioned before because they were not condemned. The preoccupation of the Talmud with them may indicate that they were something the Jewish Diaspora encountered in the Roman World. Was *coitus interruptus* so obvious a device that even writers who give comprehensive counsel on birth-control omitted

[5] A native of New Guinea has been known to advocate it on these grounds. Havelock Ellis, *Studies in the Psychology of Sex I* (1897), p. 4.

[6] Believed to have been responsible for the heavy fall in the birth-rate in France at the end of the eighteenth century and the beginning of the nineteenth. J. Peel and M. Potts, *Textbook of Contraceptive Practice* (1969), pp. 49–51.

it? Or was it in fact unknown (for Professor Keith Hopkins has pointed out that it is unknown today in some primitive societies that practise other forms of birth-control)?

There is a well-known passage in Lucretius in which he says that certain modes of intercourse promote fertility whereas others inhibit it, and ascribes to prostitutes what he called 'soft motions' designed to promote the client's pleasure and to prevent conception, being careful to add that they are irrelevant to wives. But he had recourse to a metaphor (from ploughing), and it is not clear just what he has in mind. His mention of prostitutes is a reminder that the oldest profession in the world must have evolved and disseminated a mass of empirical lore on birth-control, some of it perhaps quite effective.

The lore of the rhythm or safe period was also canvassed in antiquity. Soranus, the greatest ancient authority on birth-control, a Greek living at Rome about AD 100, mistakenly advised avoidance of coitus immediately before and after menstruation. The effectiveness of so-called safe periods would be extremely difficult to check without the keeping of a careful diary and without statistics drawn from a number of cases. Anyone trying this method would have discovered by bitter experience that it is full of pitfalls, as recent research has shown.

Plato, less severe in the *Republic* than he was to show himself in the *Laws*, allows his guardians free love-making after the age-period prescribed for procreation, provided they either do not 'bring to the light' anything so conceived, or dispose of it if they cannot prevent its birth. And when discussing in the *Laws* the necessity

31

for married couples to limit the sons they support to one, he remarks that there are many methods of birth-control. That passage in the *Republic* is referring euphemistically to infanticide and abortion, the methods of family planning most frequently mentioned in antiquity, to which we may now turn.

Infanticide in the form of the exposure of infants was deeply rooted in Greek mythology even in legends of infant gods, from Zeus downwards, being exposed but rescued, as well as heroes and heroines. Apart from Oedipus, the most famous cases in literature were Ion (the eponymous hero of Euripides' play, which like all his plays reflects contemporary questions) and Daphnis and Chloe (in Longus' pastoral romance). What evidence is there that it was practised in historical times, apart from the eugenic provisions already mentioned (for the literary tales of foundlings *could* be merely variations on a romantic tradition)?

We know that it was authorised by the early law of Gortyn in Crete, and the only law against it that we know of, from Thebes, is probably as late as the Antonine Age. A casual reference in Plato's *Theaetetus* may be none the less significant for being a metaphor: 'Let us inspect this argument and see if it is worth rearing.' At the end of this dialogue Socrates, who has adopted the role of midwife of ideas, concludes: 'All of this *the midwife's skill* pronounces to be mere windeggs and *not worth rearing*' (Cornford). It is unlikely that Plato would have proposed infanticide as a regular feature of his *Republic* without comment if he and his readers had not been callous through familiarity with it; and, likewise, casual references in the comic poets give the impression that it was not an idea which would be horrifically unfamiliar to the audience. Of course it may well have been commoner in the case of the bastard offspring of slave girls and courtesans than of married couples.

For the Hellenistic Age more concrete evidence comes from inscriptions, in the form of a wholly unnatural predominance in numbers of males over females. Despite war casualties, there were usually, it appears, more males than females in antiquity. It is true that—partly because of inferiority in women's diet, partly because of deaths in childbirth made commoner by premature marriage—a female's life expectancy was five to ten years shorter than a male's. But the preponderance requires more explanation than that, and must largely be attributed to infanticide. There is no doubt that a prejudice against daughters existed, due partly to unwillingness to pay their eventual dowry. Stobaeus collected a number of quotations that illustrate it: for instance, 'Everyone, even if poor, raises a son, but even if rich, exposes a daughter.' Injunctions by a departing father to a pregnant wife to rear her child if it proves to be male but not if it proves to be female, which we find in fiction in Terence and Apuleius, are paralleled from real life in a papyrus fragment.

But more telling are figures collected by Sir William Tarn of some Hellenistic families. At Delphi in the second century BC out of 600 families only 1 per cent reared more than one daughter. This result could only be produced artificially, for two sons occur quite often. Also, in general, families were preternaturally small. Five was the biggest Tarn could find, with one exception of seven, in the Hellenistic Age. (The modern Chinese claim to have found a technique for diagnosing the sex of an unborn child. It was reported in 1975 that in fifty-three cases where a boy was identified and abortion offered this was accepted in only one, whereas in forty-six cases where a girl was identified it was accepted in twenty-nine.)

In Rome the *paterfamilias* had the right to decide whether any child in his *familia* should be reared. There are some famous decisions. Augustus ordered the exposure of the daughter of his wayward granddaughter Julia, Claudius of that of his adulterous and divorced wife Urgulanilla. Tacitus alleged the non-existence of birth-control among the Germans as part of their exemplary innocence, but the prohibition of infanticide by the Jews as one of their characteristic eccentricities. His moral ambivalence does not weaken the implication that the practice was common in Rome. Sir Ronald Syme has suggested that the lack of known bastards among the Roman aristocracy (or even of imputations of bastardy in the unrestrained invectives of the late Republic) is evidence that they were suppressed. But of course in many cases they could simply have sunk into the plebeian unknown. It is a curious anomaly that the word *spurius*, meaning 'bastard', occurs only in post-classical Latin; yet as a proper name it is quite common from early times. (Macaulay, if not his 'schoolboy', had heard of Spurius Lartius, who kept the bridge with Horatius.)

As to methods of suppression, though strangling, drowning and other violent devices were employed (no doubt through the agency of menials in the case of the wealthier), a reluctance actually to kill was, not unnaturally, common: exposure was less immediate. The baby simply had to be got rid of. The heart-break of the mothers is the most miserable part of the whole affair, touchingly exhibited in Creusa in Euripides' *Ion*. It might seek mitigation in fancies of pious dedication of the offspring to a god: hence perhaps the frequent choice of a temple or holy cave as the place of deposit.

In Rome there was an idea that the exposing of babies could expiate a prodigy; and on the death of the adored prince Germanicus mothers exposed their babies as a token of mourning. But often parents hoped the child would survive. Town babies were left less often in remote places haunted by beasts and birds of prey than in streets or markets; in Athens, for instance, in the Cynosarge Gymnasium, in Rome beneath a particular column near the Velabrum, where passers-by were most likely to find them. They were also left there shortly before dawn, to give them the maximum period of daylight in which to be found. They were not only provided with toys and trinkets to comfort them, if need be, in the next world, but sometimes bound with wreaths and fillets, protective charms, and placed well wrapped up in a basket or pot. Someone might be left to watch and report if the child was found, like Moses' sister in the Bible.

Though a finder's first reaction might be one of revulsion, there were some reasons why babies might actually be sought. A childless couple might simply want to bring up a child, or a woman might seek to attach a former lover by confronting him with his supposed offspring. Rearing as slaves might seem a more probable motive. We are told that Megarians in particular sought babies at Athens for this purpose. There was a certain amount of white slave traffic for the Asiatic market. In Rome, Gaius Melissus (a talented member of Maecenas' circle) had been exposed because his parents were at loggerheads, and subsequently brought up as a slave. When his mother tried to reclaim him, he preferred to remain a slave in such exalted company.

But slaves were expensive to rear; and until the Roman era of conquest came to an end, and with it the influx of foreign captives, it may not have been particularly profitable to do so. Another deterrent was the rule that the natural parents could reclaim their children if they could be recognised and if the children themselves consented. Those accompanying objects, even if not primarily intended to facilitate recognition, have played their part in recognition scenes in fiction from those of Euripides' Ion to Miss Prism's handbag. Trajan, consulted by Pliny and unable to find established case-law in his archives, ruled that freeborn foundlings, if identified, should be freed from slavery without payment.

It was a general softening of feeling combined with continuing anxiety about manpower in the Roman Empire that induced Nerva and Trajan to institute schemes for the support of poor children. The foundling hospitals and orphanages of eighteenth and early nineteenth-century Europe were often little better than organised infanticide; but the spread of contraception, and more recently of legalised abortion, has meant that our orphanages and adoption agencies can now cope with what was a major problem in antiquity.

Infanticide had two advantages over abortion. First, it was safer for the mother; and secondly you knew before deciding its fate the sex of the child. Was there no prejudice against infanticide in the pagan world? In some communities there was; for Aristotle said that surplus (as distinct from deformed) infants should not be got rid of by exposure if the established customs of a state forbade it. In such states recourse must be had to abortion. But it is not until the first century AD that we find infanticide specifically condemned in extant writing, by the Alexandrian Jew Philo and the Roman Stoic Musonius Rufus.

As to abortion, the methods advocated in antiquity are listed by Keith Hopkins:

> Anything ranging from a surgical operation of the knitting needle variety, malnutrition and inanition of the foetus, and the use of purgatives, diuretics, emetics, pessaries and aciduous medicaments, to direct pressure on the body, punching, lifting heavy weights, jumping, and riding in a cart along rough roads, together with the inevitable magical recipes, potions and lapidaries.

The dangers were of course considerable, and were publicised by such incidents as the death of Domitia, compelled to abort by her uncle, the Emperor Domitian, who had seduced her.

Whether or not abortion was illegal in Athens is a moot point. There was a speech ascribed to the fourth-century orator Lysias which turned on the question. But it is hard to believe that Plato and Aristotle would have prescribed it without self-defensive argument for their ideal states had it been illegal, or even generally considered outrageous. The Hippocratic Oath did indeed abjure facilitating it in any way. But that was in the context of the physician's overriding duty, which we find later formulated by Soranus, to preserve what nature engenders; and it may also have been a precaution against the dangerous nature of some drugs purveyed as abortifacients. Nor was that oath ever official, even if taken at all. Embryectomy was disapproved of by the most reputable doctors unless the life of the mother would otherwise be in danger. The first specific condemnation of abortion in a moral context occurs in an inscription of about 100 BC from a private shrine at Lydian Philadelphia. Of course it was a crime for a wife to abort without telling her husband: that was an infringement of his right to determine family planning. This applied even if divorce had intervened.

In the Roman world abortion seems to have been commonly practised, but more by crude manipulation than by potions. The sale of abortifacients was illegal, and those who purveyed them were treated as poisoners. Ovid's well-known protest should not be taken too seriously. In a pair of poems in his *Amores* he represents his Corinna as having induced an abortion surgically. His violent reaction is due to concern for her safety, so indirectly is an expression of love. He inveighs against abortion in general, but in his usual rhetorical manner, ingeniously deploying all the arguments he can think of to discredit it. Anyone who knows his Ovid will not take this as evidence of Roman law, or even opinion. But there are signs of disapproval in others, including Cicero. Seneca praised his mother for not having practised abortion like other women, which is interesting, since strictly speaking it was the *paterfamilias* who would decide. It shows that in practice the mother would have her say. We may take it that abortion was something deprecated in respectable circles, whose prevalence however was taken for granted.

Aristotle, too, had made an important reservation: abortion must not take place if life has begun in the embryo. That he reckoned, following contemporary medical opinion, to be on the fortieth day for males, on the ninetieth for females. This is still considered by many to be the crux. Ancient opinion varied as to whether the soul entered at conception, at birth, or at some intermediate stage. It was debated whether the foetus could be called a living entity, or whether it was simply part of its mother. But the opinion that prevailed so far as to become the basis of Roman law on the subject was that of the Stoics: that the foetus was part of the mother, and that the soul did not enter until the moment of contact with the outside air. This was very important: it meant that a woman who aborted could not be deemed a murderess. Today a common criterion is that abortion should not take place after the foetus is capable of surviving delivery.[7]

[7] Our present British law provides that a child may not be destroyed by abortion (except to save the mother's life) if it is capable of surviving after delivery, and there is a presumption that it *is* capable of surviving after the twenty-eighth week. But a healthy child may have some chance of surviving from several weeks before that, in which event its abortion would be unlawful. The Lane Committee proposed that the presumption of viability should be lowered to the twenty-fourth, and Mr James White's private member's bill to the twentieth, to allow for mistakes in the dates; but the law at present remains unchanged.

Contraceptive devices were also prescribed by ancient medical writers, though not much space is allotted to them in the handbooks, and there is surprisingly no reference to them in the Third Book of Ovid's *Art of Love*, which gives the woman's side. There was a tendency not to distinguish them from abortifacients. Soranus, who was clear on the distinction, stressed the advantages of the former over the latter. Potions were the commonest form, the only one mentioned in the Hippocratic Corpus; and a hundred plants from which they could be distilled are mentioned by one writer or another. N. E. Himes, in his pioneering *Medical History of Contraception* (1936), dismissed them as undoubtedly ineffective, since no drug was known to Western science that, taken orally, would prevent conception. That was in 1936, just two years before the discovery that eventually led to 'The Pill'. Condoms were unknown in the ancient world. They are first mentioned by Gabriele Faloppio in 1564, as made of linen, and were used by Casanova among others. But they did not become at all common until the first vulcanisation of rubber in 1844.

There were, however, vaginal plugs and occlusive pessaries, first mentioned in Aristotle. These were of wool smeared with various substances, such as myrtle oil and white lead, honey, cedar-gum, alum or peppermint. The rationale was not necessarily understood. Thus Aristotle thought it was the *smoothness* of the oil instead of its stickiness that might be effective. Sticky substances can hold up spermatazoa (Marie Stopes was still advocating olive oil in 1931). Others of the substances recommended do have some spermicidal effect, such as vinegar, lemon juice, and alum. But it must have been well-nigh impossible to prove positive effectiveness. Some man, sterile by nature, might mistakenly but enthusiastically point to the manifest efficacy in his case even of one or other of the magic amulets which were also freely prescribed by pundits of lower calibre than Soranus.

It is odd that, while Greek had a specific noun for contraceptive, *atokion,* Latin had none beyond *venenum* ('poison'). And the scarcity of clear mention of any in Roman writers probably indicates general lack of confidence in them rather than their being so common as to be taken for granted. As to specific disapproval, it is found again in Musonius Rufus.

But when all is said and done, a mystery remains: how was it that so many men whom we know, or must believe, to have positively wanted a legitimate male heir, including Julius Caesar and Augustus, failed to produce one?

Finally, what was the attitude to these matters of the early Christians? As to population, the Old Testament injunctions to increase and multiply had been abandoned by the Jews after the Diaspora in favour of the two-child family deemed sufficient for the continuance of the race. Philo and Musonius both considered that sexual intercourse even within marriage was wrong unless aimed at procreation.[8] This doctrine, rooted in Stoic and perhaps Jewish puritanism, anticipated that of many Fathers of the Church. It is noteworthy that Constantine annulled the often re-enacted Augustan legislation for promoting the birth-rate. The Christian

[8] Jerome cites Seneca as saying, 'let men show themselves to their wives not as lovers but as husbands'.

41

doctrine on marriage itself, developed from the New Testament in the context of belief in 'the shortness of the time' before the second coming, was that it was not unacceptable, but inferior to celibacy in holiness;[9] and this took precedence over any doctrine of political expediency.

Infanticide and abortion were condemned by Christians from the earliest times, again anticipated by Philo and Musonius. But Tertullian and St Augustine allowed abortion where otherwise the foetus could become the unwitting murderer of its mother. Otherwise St Augustine condemned married couples who practised infanticide, abortion or the use of 'sterility poisons' (presumably contraceptives).[10] He also condemned the Manichaean use of the so-called sterile period, and unfruitful modes of intercourse in general, adding 'That is what Onan, son of Judah did, and God killed him for it.' Actually the sin of Onan was his frustration of Judah's injunction that he should beget children by his brother's widow, not the method by which he did it. But the mistaken interpretation given to Genesis 38, 8–10, by some Rabbis and St Augustine was perpetuated by St Jerome in the way he translated

[9] In the Church of England marriage service, the second reason given for the ordaining of marriage is 'for a remedy against sin and to avoid fornication; that such persons as have not the gift of continency might marry and keep themselves undefiled members of Christ's body'.

[10] *Marriage and Concupiscence* 1.15.17. Under the title '*Aliquando*' this has been the prime text in the Catholic condemnation of contraceptives. The condemnation of all artificial forms of birth-control was reaffirmed by St Thomas Aquinas in his *Summa Theologiae*, by Pope Sixtus V in his bull *Effrenatum* of 1588, and by Pope Paul VI in his encyclical *Humanae Vitae* of 1968.

the passage in the Vulgate, with the appalling result that what became known as 'onanism' was branded for all Christendom as a sin, and one worthy of the severest condemnation.

The Christians did eventually compensate for their severe attitude towards pagan methods of family planning by what was called 'the patrimony of the poor'. Constantine, instigated by Lactantius, made much more general the schemes of some previous emperors for the nurture and clothing of poor children. Official foundling hospitals were slow to develop because of fears that they would be an encouragement to fornication.[11] But many exposed infants seem to have been reared by individual Christians.

And on this more cheerful note I will end what has been, I am afraid, a rather sordid story, but one for lack of which accounts of ancient life have too often been inadequate.

[11] Cf. the fears aroused, especially in our non-conformist churches, when a cure was found for syphilis.

TWO

II

Women's Liberation

HOW can I keep up my zeal for the cause?' a suffragette asked Mrs Pankhurst. 'Trust in God,' came the reply, 'She will help you.' The fact that this can pass as a joke with us shows how deeply we are impregnated with patriarchal assumptions. Milton put this attitude in a nutshell:

He for God only, she for God in him.

The modern movement for women's liberation began in the climate that produced the French Revolution and Tom Paine's *Rights of Man*. Its standard-bearer, at any rate for English-speaking people, was Mary Wollstonecraft, whose *Vindication of the Rights of Women* appeared in the revolutionary year of 1792. Claire Tomalin has summed up her views as follows:

Woman are human beings before they are sexual beings; mind has no sex; society is wasting its assets if it retains women in the role of convenient domestic slaves and 'alluring mistresses', denies them economic independence, and encourages them to be attentive to their looks to the exclusion of all else.[1]

But she also held a view not unknown in antiquity, that sexuality was wrong in itself, redeemed only by parenthood, and largely imposed on women by men. She spoke disapprovingly of husbands who 'seduce' their wives, and expressed the view that it is better for marriage to exclude passionate love.

That other year of revolution, 1848, saw the inauguration in America of an organised 'Woman's Movement', sparked off by the agitation for the abolition of slavery. A coherent philosophy was provided by John Stuart Mill's *The Subjection of Women* of 1869. Three years earlier the first petition for women's suffrage had been presented to our British Parliament. More than fifty years were to pass before it was granted; and when it was, that was allegedly due less to the pre-War agitation and violence of the suffragettes than to the fact that women, having had to be employed in wartime to undertake work normally done by men, had proved their capacity. But perhaps this explanation was just a male face-saver.

It was, however, only a fractional victory. Indeed the period 1930 to 1960 was in some respects reactionary. It is only within the past few years that women and their supporters have returned to the charge, storming such citadels as the more adventurous colleges of Cambridge, and later of Oxford; the Queen's Bench; the Stock Exchange; and the leadership of the Conservative Party. And books such as

[1] *The Life and Death of Mary Wollstonecraft*, Weidenfeld and Nicolson, 1974.

Kate Millet's *Sexual Politics* (1969) in America and Germaine Greer's *The Female Eunuch* (1970) in Britain have preached the far more fundamental revolution heralded by Friedrich Engels—not only equality of rights, opportunity and pay between the sexes, but the abandonment of the patriarchal family as the social unit together with the image of the wife as passive partner and ministering angel. 1975, nominated as 'Women's Year', at least saw the passing of the Sex Discrimination Act; but to this type of feminist that has seemed merely inadequate reformism.

Anything so extreme as this is rarely to be found in the Greek and Roman worlds of antiquity. Indeed the overall impression is of a man's world in which women were relegated to a life of seclusion. The Greeks were however, aware that just outside the Hellenic periphery there were peoples among whom the social roles of men and women were reversed or where women were dominant; in Egypt, for instance (though this was in fact no longer so when Herodotus and Sophocles were writing), and in parts of Asia Minor.[2]

What approaches were there in the classical world, either in theory or practice, in the sphere of law, politics, society or the inner life of the individual, to 'women's liberation'?

Three things we must bear in mind all the time. First,

[2] According to Herodotus Lydian girls, having earned the amount of a dowry by prostitution, gave their hand in marriage to whomever they wished. The Lycians honoured women more than men, took their names from their mothers, and passed their inheritance to daughters, not sons. If a Lycian woman married a foreigner or slave, their children were free citizens.

that Athens, through the survival of her massive dramatic, historical and oratorical literature, is the only Greek state of which we have really detailed knowledge, though we have interesting information about Sparta, and much detail from papyri, supplemented by literature, about the Hellenised part of Ptolemaic Egypt. Secondly, that the literature was produced almost entirely by men. And thirdly, that we know very little about the poor, whose struggle for existence tends to produce a life-style of ubiquitous similarity. As Aristotle said, the poor man, having no slaves, was obliged to use his wife and children as servants, and no magistrate could prevent the wives of the poor from going around out of doors. They could at least gossip at the well.

In Homer women are not secluded. Helen can walk on the walls of Troy; the princess Nausicaä can take her washing down to the beach with her companions; young men and girls can have loving talk together (as Hector recalls when he turns finally to face Achilles). The marriage state is idealised, but it is one in which the provinces of the partners are already clearly divided (as Hector gently reminds Andromache when she tries to advise him on tactics in fighting). Wives have no place even at the dining-table, only in the household, at the loom, and in the marriage-bed. A woman's beauty and accomplishments are a status-symbol won by her husband, though she in turn receives reflected glory from his prestige. Arete, Queen of Phaeacia, may seem an exception, and indeed she was one that proved the rule; for Athena herself says that King Alcinoüs honours her as no other woman anywhere in the whole world is honoured. But hers is a personal influence, exercised through him, on whom, it is expressly said, 'all the power and might of the Phaeacians depend'.

Penelope's case is peculiar. Her husband is missing, but not known to be dead. There is confusion as to whether, if once he is presumed dead, it is for her father Icarius or for her son Telemachus (once he comes of age) to decide who next may marry her. But what is clear is that even a Queen has a male in the position of guardian (*kyrios*), whether husband, father, or son. We also find in Homer a double standard of sexual morality. A male may go to bed with females other than his wife, either simply for pleasure or to get himself a male heir (as Menelaus did by amicable arrangement with Helen, who had not provided him with one); but a wife was expected to remain faithful, even if in this age the burden of opprobrium fell more heavily on an adulterer than an adulteress, on Paris than Helen. And even the gods, as Calypso complains, are jealous if a goddess takes a mortal as bedfellow, sometimes to the extent of killing him. Calypso's complaint is the first protest in the struggle for equal rights for women (even if it is not enough to justify Samuel Butler's belief that the *Odyssey* was composed by a woman).

When Greece re-emerged from its Dark Age there survived from Homeric times these three features: the guardian without whom no woman could perform any legal act; the restriction of wives' chief occupations to working wool, spinning and weaving, and the supervision of the household slaves; and the double standard of sexual morality. At the same time we find in Hesiod's myth of Pandora and her jar full of evils the beginning of an un-Homeric tradition in literature of male vituperation or mockery of women in which genuine misogyny merged into rhetorical and satirical virtuosity,[3] culminating in the 660 vitriolic lines of Juvenal's Sixth Satire. The reflection that wives are a regrettable necessity, useful only for producing legitimate offspring, occurs to men ranging from Euripides' Jason and Hippolytus to the Roman censor Metellus Macedonicus.

In Sappho's Lesbos and other Aegean isles, in some Dorian and aristocratic states in the so-called archaic period round about 600 BC, and among the Greeks of Sicily and South Italy, we glimpse a life in which women were socially free, as in Homer. But the general pattern seems to have become that of the democratic city-state of which Athens is the supreme example. (I say 'seems' because for the classical period we know too little about states other than Athens.)

The former comparative freedom of aristocratic ladies was suppressed. Of course women had no political role: it was more than a nine-days'-wonder when a woman of the pan-Hellenic colony of Thurii in South Italy succeeded in addressing the Assembly. The whole point of the first half of Aristophanes' play *Ecclesiazusae* (*The Women's Assembly*) was that the idea was utterly paradoxical, a *reductio ad absurdum*: men had made such a mess of things that women could hardly do worse—though even an Athenian male chauvinist must have felt a grudging admiration for their organiser, Praxagora, still more for Lysistrata

[3] E.g. 'There are only two happy days in a husband's life, his wedding-day and his wife's funeral.' (Falsely attributed to Hipponax.)

(who in the war-time play of that name tries to get the wives of Athens and Sparta to blackmail their husbands into making peace by denying them their sexual expectations). Women could in reality play a part behind the scenes. A wife of strong personality could influence a sensible or a weaker husband. It is a striking fact that one reason for which an Athenian could be held incompetent at law—along with constraint, senility, disease, and the influence of drugs—was being under the persuasion of a woman.

In Athenian law a woman's male guardian, whether father, husband, father's legitimate or testamentary heir (in that order) or failing these a public official, the *archon*, could dispose of her in marriage or adoption, and even in theory sell her into slavery if she was caught being seduced. Normally a girl passed from the guardianship of her father, who fixed up a marriage for her when she was fourteen, into that of her husband; but her father, or failing him her agnate next-of-kin, retained the right to get the *archon* to dissolve the marriage. Her dowry was all-important; but it did not belong to her, for a woman could own no property. It remained part of the estate of her father's family; and at the wedding her husband had to sign an inventory. Thenceforward he had the usufruct, and this passed to their children.

But he did not have things all his own way. Divorce was easy, and whatever the cause, the dowry reverted. The wife thus had some security as against lack of freedom: her husband could not afford to maltreat her intolerably. He was also bound by law to support her, as were her children after his death. If she was left a widow, she reverted to the guardianship of her father or agnate next-of-kin, and anyone could prosecute a guardian who failed to do his legal duty. But many widows were young enough to remarry. Thus every woman in Athens who wanted it had a man's roof to live under. The state also tried to ensure that as many of its women citizens as possible had a husband. This would be an effect, if it was not a primary motive, of Pericles' law of 451 BC by which children of citizens married to alien wives were not to be citizens. The state provided dowries for girls who could not afford one but were attractive enough to find suitors.

Adultery involving a citizen's wife was treated as a very serious crime, and not merely because it outraged male *amour propre*. It was considered essential that the paternity of children should not be in doubt, not only because of the husband's feelings towards them, but because a main reason for the care taken to ensure the perpetuation of citizen families was the maintenance by each of the religious cult of its ancestors, and there must be no interloper. If an *archon* failed in his duty of seeing that a family had a male heir, it was for impiety that he was prosecuted. On the other hand, intercourse by husbands with non-citizens had no such serious result; and it was tolerated provided the wife, the security for the dowry, was not made (as she was in the case of Alcibiades) to take second place. Nor was there anything to prevent a man from enjoying a slave in his own household. It is significant that one feature of the women's paradise proclaimed by Aristophanes' Praxagora is that slave-girls will not compete with free wives in matters of love.

Such a state of affairs is worlds away from that advocated by our feminists; but it must be seen in the
context of the democratic city-state.

The city was what gave meaning to its citizens' lives.
The inclinations of individuals had to be sacrificed for
the common feeling of well-being. The city was an
aggregate of families, not individuals. These laws were
directed to the preservation of families through the
provision of legitimate male heirs. The disregard of the
mother's family, however misguided it may seem, was
not irrational male chauvinism. The common belief
was that genetic inheritance resided in the male seed,
the female providing little more than a passive matrix,
as Apollo affirms in Aeschylus' *Eumenides*; and indeed
the function of the ovum in mammalian genetics was
not understood until the nineteenth century. A family
could therefore be truly perpetuated only in the male
line.

As to social life for female citizens, everything was
motivated by fear of adultery. Women of the classes
above the poverty line lived in a secluded part of the
dull house behind locked doors. Any tendency to personal display was stifled by Solon's sumptuary laws.
They were not present when anyone other than rela-
tives came to a meal, nor did they go out to meals or
parties with their husbands; in fact they rarely went out
at all, apart from a walk with a female slave in
attendance, except to a family reunion or a religious
festival. They plied household tasks in the company of
female slaves. Men on the other hand were out all day,
in the Assembly, or law-court or gymnasium, working
or doing the household shopping, or conversing in
some colonnade or at a party. Women were generally

regarded as a different kind of human being, complementary to men. One has only to recall the single sentence addressed to them at the end of Pericles' funeral oration in Thucydides:

> Great will be your glory if you are found not inferior to your nature; and the greatest of all is hers who is least spoken of by men, whether for praise or blame.

Xenophon's Ischomachus, an idealised Athenian country gentleman, married a girl of fifteen properly brought up to speak, hear, and see as little as possible. Her role was to supervise the household and to obey her father and her husband, who regarded himself as a sort of bird-tamer.

Aristotle, at the end of the classical period, though he deprecates the way that some barbarians treat their wives as slaves, is yet convinced that women are intellectually, physically and morally inferior to men, and that it is natural for men to rule and women to obey. No wonder that women took to drink, as the comedians liked to allege.

Whether they attended the theatrical performances or not is disputed. It seems most probable that they did, and that would not be out of keeping, since these were originally religious festivals, in honour of Dionysus.

And the mention of the theatre recalls doubts that have been raised about the orthodox conception of their life. In three of Aristophanes' plays they are represented as knowing quite a lot about politics (*Lysistrata*), quite a lot about the latest social theories (*Ecclesiazusae*), and quite a lot about Euripides (*Thesmophoriazusae*). That could, of course, be part of the humorous paradox, but it seems more significant; and we know from casual evidence, from law-suits for instance, that husbands did discuss public affairs with their wives. Again, the tragedies are full of female characters who are far from cloistered, though often, especially in Euripides, they apologise for their unfeminine boldness and show respect for the conventional limitations of the poet's day. Some (such as Clytemnestra, Medea, and Antigone) are represented as having the spirit of a man; the daring Electra is contrasted with her normal sister Chrysothemis; and Antigone at least could scarcely fail to excite a measure of sympathy and admiration. Admittedly the audience would be conscious that these were Queens and Princesses, inhabiting a distant world, as a Russian audience of today must feel when viewing a nineteenth-century opera. Yet such plays, especially those of Euripides, must have given an audience as intelligent as the Athenians food for thought about its preconceptions, and contributed to the so-called Sophistic Enlightenment of the late fifth century.

Human beings are apt to behave in practice more humanely than their theories and institutions would suggest. The Attic vase-paintings of 470–430 are full of interest in family life. The funeral vases, like the funeral monuments, depict in a most moving way farewells between husband and wife. It is a commonplace that arranged marriages may lead to mutual affection, perhaps no less often than marriages originating in romantic passion. In any case it would be wrong to assume that the average Athenian looked down on his wife. Even Xenophon's Ischomachus treats his at least as a partner in running the estate and bringing up the children; and even Aristotle dearly loved his wife Pytheas. An Attic orator of the fourth century remarked glibly before a jury,

> We resort to courtesans for our pleasures, keep concubines to minister to our daily comforts, and marry wives to give us legitimate children and be faithful guardians of our domestic hearths.

But the demarcation lines were not as clear as that. Sophocles' *Trachiniae* is about a wife's attempt to win back her husband's love from a new concubine. Xenophon, at the end of his *Symposium,* has the guests, mildly excited by a boy and girl cabaret whose climax was a kiss, jump on their horses and gallop home to their wives. And the mainspring of the *Lysistrata* is that the men suffer terrible deprivation from the sexual strike of their wives: it is only in ultimate desperation that they talk of resorting to prostitutes, though state brothels had long since been instituted by Solon.

But if we are thinking of women's liberation as it is conceived of today, it must be something more than security with a good chance of affection within a confining patriarchal system in which citizenship was the paramount value. What about the concubines and courtesans of that orator's dictum?

A concubine could be a lower-class Athenian, an immigrant, or a slave. The Greeks were monogamous, and no doubt a wife was enough for most citizens. But a man might like to keep a concubine also, if he could square or dupe his wife and children. Sometimes however this broke up the marriage. Alcibiades' wife sought to leave him because he brought his mistresses home. Pericles, on the other hand, married off his wife to someone else, leaving himself free to take on later as concubine the Milesian courtesan Aspasia. More often, perhaps, it would be a case of a widower consoling himself with a favourite slave, whom he would set free. Or a courtesan might be glad to retire into the greater security of concubinage. Aristotle, after his wife's death, had an intimate relationship with the courtesan Herpyllis, mother of Nicomachus, for the rest of his life, and provided for her in his will. The line between wife and concubine at Athens was very thin; and whereas the superior status of the wife must be kept clear, the concubine might have more freedom. Also, instead of providing a dowry (and this was the crux of the matter) she was provided for. Nevertheless to keep a concubine when you have a wife seems to have been considered an un-Greek trait, not really respectable.

A woman might become a concubine either because she was a slave and had to, or to better herself, or for love. Timandra, the mistress of Alcibiades, stuck to him when he was outlawed and gave him the best burial she could afford. She was the mother of the famous courtesan Lais, who set all Greece on fire and was the favourite model of Apelles. I have used the old-fashioned word 'courtesan' to represent the Greek *hetaera* (companion), a woman who, although she sold her sexual favours, studied to educate herself so that her arts and conversation might also make her agreeable to men. Socrates in Xenophon expresses surprise at finding the house of the *hetaera* Theodota so elegant.

So far from being forbidden to attend men's parties, such women were often the chief attraction of them, and they were mainly sought by young, unmarried men. It is these *demi-mondaines*, often adventuresses from abroad, who come nearest to being liberated women in the modern sense.

And yet—not everyone would enjoy the life even of the famous Thais, in Menander's words 'loving no one but always pretending', not to mention progressively lowering one's sights as the years went by, charging less, and accepting older men. *Hetaerae* are represented by the orators as pleasant but scandalous parasites. They were not protected by the law; and it was hard for them to save up for a dreaded old age when land, the safest investment, could not be held by women. The best hope was to be taken on as concubine of a man of substance, which incidentally secured exemption from the tax on prostitution. But that might still leave you stranded if he got tired of you or died. The opposite of wives, these women had a sort of freedom in place of security. The fourth century was the great age of the *grandes cocottes*, glorified in the so-called Middle Comedy.

Let me turn now for a moment from Athens to Sparta. There the picture is very different.

An aristocratic tradition was maintained by the narrow oligarchy of 'Spartiate' peers, who were above all a military caste. They had to be that if they were to keep in subjection the Helots and Messenians on whose labour they depended. So they became for Athenian aristocrats the ideal of a state which had *eunomia*, law and order, without the besetting curse of most Greek

cities, class warfare. There is admittedly an element
of myth in the conception of her institutions, attributed to the old lawgiver Lycurgus and later
enshrined in Plutarch's Life of him, and some of the
stories it generated may only have been *ben trovato*.
But Plato and Xenophon knew Sparta at the height of
her success, in the first thirty years of the fourth
century, after her victory in the Peloponnesian War;
and they can hardly have misrepresented her institutions in essentials.

As to women, the emphasis was on producing sturdy
spear-fodder. To a foreigner who remarked that only
Spartan women ruled their men Leonidas' wife is said
to have replied, 'We alone produce men.' According to
Plutarch, no Spartan women had her name inscribed on
a tombstone unless she died in childbirth. Far from
being cloistered to protect their chastity, girls did
gymnastic training with boys, to the scandal of other
Greeks. They danced in each other's presence naked,
or perhaps lightly clad, allegedly to promote desire for
marriage. This is the more surprising as a reason—
since girls were not married, as they were elsewhere,
when physically still immature. For eugenic purposes both bride and groom had to be in the prime of
life.

We are told about an institution of trial marriage, for
which there are at any rate parallels. For some time a
couple, secretly engaged, would meet and have intercourse clandestinely, the youth returning for the night
to his barracks. If the girl conceived, they would get
married; if not, it was quietly broken off and no one
was any the wiser. Such was the desire to produce
numerous enough and sturdy enough pure-bred

Spartiates that, as we saw, wife-sharing was quite in order,[4] concubinage being practically unknown and prostitution rare. Men did not set up house till they were about thirty, and home life meant little. Their children were looked after by slaves; boys were taken away from home at seven and initiated into mess life, being regarded as children of the state; and even the spinning and weaving were not done by wives, again in striking contrast to other Greek communities, but by servants.

Spartiate women were consequently a leisured class, save that they had more responsible duties undertaken elsewhere by men. Their husbands were so often and so long absent on campaign, and when at home so occupied with military training and security duties, that they did not themselves farm estates. A good deal of management had to be entrusted to their wives. Women at Sparta were submitted to no guardian. They were nearer in age to their husbands than in Athens, for instance. They owned and drove horses. More important, they could own land; and by Aristotle's time more than two-fifths of the Spartan homeland, Laconia, was in their hands. Heiresses made acquisitive marriages, their correspondingly heavy dowries impoverishing the rest of their family. Spartiate women emerged more powerful than ever from the long Peloponnesian War.

Aristotle noted the paradox that in war-like peoples the women tend to rule the men. So it was in Sparta (even though the Kings and magistrates were males). Wives were addressed as 'mistress'. These women came near in some ways to the liberated women of modern times. But they had too little to do. Conditioned like

[4] Timaea, wife of King Agis of Sparta, was proud to have a son by Alcibiades.

Hitlermädchen to breed soldiers for a repressive
police-state, they were (as Plato observed) inade-
quately equipped for leisure. When Sparta, in relief and
elation at her victory, relaxed her traditional discipline,
she found too late that it was impossible psychologi-
cally to reimpose it. This applied specially to the
women, who proved a liability in the crisis of Sparta's
undoing at the Battle of Leuctra in 371.

But in the rest of Greece also preconceptions about
women, as about everything else, began to loosen up in
the so-called Sophistic Enlightenment of the late fifth
century, even if in the short run the reactionaries prevailed against such advanced spirits as Socrates and
Euripides. This movement was probably accelerated
by the fact that prolonged absence of men on campaign
had the same effect on women's importance as at
Sparta; also that the death of so many men in war made
women preponderate in numbers. But even earlier, in
the second quarter of the fifth century, vase paintings
show a marked increase of interest in women.
Euripides went so far as to make one of his characters
say that while there was nothing worse than a bad
woman, there was nothing better than a good one; and
he exemplified a good one as a wife in his *Alcestis*.

It seems to have been Socrates who propounded the
novel thesis, taken up by many after him, that good
(arete) is the same in woman as in man. The character of
Aspasia, admired in the Socratic circle, may have
brought this home to open-minded thinkers. A pupil
of Socrates called Aeschines of Sphettos composed,
about the year 386, a dialogue entitled *Aspasia*, fragments of which (if they are genuine) show that he made

some character maintain that love *(eros)* between husband and wife was the means of getting the best out of both; and that the impulse to improve one another was the essence of love, not only in the discipleship of male to male, but in the marriage relationship. Here, at last, is some approach to equality of the sexes.

A corollary was that girls ought to have the same education as boys. Plato in his *Republic* started from the premise that, childbirth apart, women differ in capacity from men only as one man differs from another, or one woman from another. It followed that women should not be confined to household chores, but should be eligible for his military élite of guardians. The only difference between a woman and a man selected would be that the woman, as being physically weaker, would be allotted lighter duties. In fact, Plato insists, this was natural, whereas the existing system of having different roles for the two sexes was unnatural. There would be no monogamous marriages, only periodic temporary couplings; and the children would be brought up as belonging to the community, unrecognisable by their natural parents. In the *Laws* he says that if one half of the state only is happy, the legislator has failed.

Plato was, however, no liberal as regards women. The only appearance of a woman in his dialogues (apart from the reported homily of Diotima in the *Symposium*) is that of poor Xanthippe, Socrates' wife, who is hustled away at the beginning of the *Phaedo* so that he may spend his last hours in talking calmly to his male friends, undisturbed by her womanish weeping. The dialogues, especially the *Timaeus*, contain many contemptuous implications and asides about women. Plato seems to have been that rarity in the Greek world, a bachelor, perhaps because he was a real homosexual (not a temporary one or part-time, as others were).

Nevertheless, in the *Laws* this bachelor reinstates marriage and makes it compulsory. Girls and women are to emerge (reluctant, it is assumed) out of their seclusion, and be submitted to mess life, separate from that of men and under a mistress, and given military training so that they may act as auxiliary soldiers in a crisis instead of crowding into the temples. Equality here hardly meant liberation. The logicality of giving women as well as men social responsibilities and duties is reaffirmed. But when it comes to finding suitable offices for them to fill, the only one we hear of is a new one, that of inspectress of marriages, open to those aged over forty. These inspectresses are to have daily meetings to report to each other any cases of married couples in the ten year period prescribed for procreation where either partner seems to be paying attention to things other than the eugenic reproductive duty solemnly enjoined at marriage; and if they fail by admonition or threats to get the offender to mend his or her ways, they are to inform the State Council with a view to severe sanctions. So marriage, instead of being regulated by private males, is to be regulated by the state through officious females. For the rest, women are apparently to be under male guardianship, as at Athens; and by abolishing the dowry, as setting up a relationship alloyed with money, Plato risked subjecting the wife still more to her husband if they failed to establish an altruistic relationship based on affection.

Aristotle was almost wholly reactionary as regards women. But there was one sect which was as radical as Plato had been, the Cynics. Diogenes, their founder, whose life spanned most of the fourth century, thought that marriage, like all social conventions, was contrary to nature and therefore bad. The truly free life involved jettisoning all conventions. For him community of women was not a feature contributing to a utopian state, but a symptom of sexual freedom, and community of children only an inevitable corollary. From his forerunner, the Socratic Antisthenes, he inherited the principle that good is the same in man and woman.

Diogenes is said to have been a misogynist, but at least he approved of no cohabitation save that of the man who persuades and the woman who is persuaded. His pupil Crates married. Four centuries later, when the Stoic philosopher Epictetus was explaining that a Cynic philosopher could not have a wife because his whole life was dedicated to being a mendicant preacher, someone interposed: 'What about Crates?' Epictetus replied that that was a quite exceptional case of passionate love, which could hardly recur. Hipparchia, the woman in question, was the first female 'drop-out' from a wealthy family—though I hesitate to claim that the word 'hippy' is derived from her name. She conceived a passion for Crates, his teaching and his way of life. She donned the coarse cloak of his sect; and if she had a 'bra', no doubt she burned it. She went out to meals with him, something only courtesans normally did with men. Though the Cynics believed in free intercourse by mutual consent, specimens of the innumerable stories about this couple, their public love-making and so on, are preserved only in Apuleius, and may simply be inventions to highlight the Cynic image. There is, however, better evidence for the story that they lent their daughter for trial periods of thirty days. Hipparchia is the best ancient analogy to one kind of modern liberated woman.

Zeno, the founder of Stoicism, thought that community of women was a natural dispensation which had come to be forgotten. True to his principle that one should live according to nature, he advocated its revival in his lost utopia *The Republic*, but only (as in Plato's) for an élite; for the rest it would be an impracticable ideal. Zeno was reputed to be homosexual. At any rate no woman was admitted to the Stoa; and Stoicism, destined to be the dominant philosophy of the Graeco-Roman world, confirmed marriage and motherhood as the role of women. But in Epicurus' garden women (including the *hetaera* Leontion, whom he favoured) were welcomed and treated on a par with men. There was no objection to sexual intercourse there, providing the disturbing passion of love was not involved. Indeed it was as students of philosophy that women most easily attained equality with men, and freedom. What these philosophers, Cynic, Stoic and Epicurean, had in common was their concern with the salvation or contentment of the individual soul. Individualism was the hallmark of the age.

But philosophy was not the basic cause of such liberalisation of the life of women as occurred in the Hellenistic Age. No real change could have come until the built-in element of totalitarianism in the city-state was weakened, and that was brought about by the conquests of Alexander.

Inter-city marriages came in, first in the federal leagues; then in Asia Minor and the islands; and finally even at Athens. Women poets and musicians travelled about, accompanied by their guardians. Girls now received primary and secondary education, and athletic training, just like boys, in some places along with them. The first woman physician we know of practised at Athens in the late fourth century. One at Pergamum practised in partnership with her husband. One in Lycia had her statue erected by the local council. There were also priestesses of the multiplying cults, who even if married had in this respect a sector of independent life and influence. Decrees were passed recording the services and benefactions of women, which Pericles would have thought most improper. In general it would seem that *de facto* women became less dependent on their guardians and more able to acquire wealth. But Athens remained more conservative than other Hellenised regions such as Egypt and Asia Minor.

The chief change, however, was in the conception of the married state itself. Though the institution of guardianship for women persisted everywhere, behind the façade they obtained more power to hold and use property. This is a symptom of a new idea of partnership. Marriage by consent, for love, also became commoner. In the Athenian New Comedy introduced by Menander towards the end of the fourth century conjugal love is a main theme; and this love is more than affection. There is here a recognition of the moral equality of the partners that shows that, in the long

run, the ideas of Socrates and Euripides have sunk in.
Again, the young poetess Erinna says that when her
friend Baucis married Aphrodite put in her heart
forgetfulness of the childish things they had
shared—Aphrodite, the goddess of sexual love, not
Hera, the official goddess of marriage. The idea of
marriage as a communion of love transcending the
separate interests of the partners is emerging.

It was this Hellenistic World, in which people were
seeking less how to promote the common good of their
city-state than how to be happy (or, at least, not
unhappy) as individuals, that captured its conquerors,
the Romans, in the second century BC.

In theory, at least, Rome still retained the institutions of a city-state. Wives were for breeding citizens. But although women had themselves no political
rights or functions, even legend of early times told of
their personal influence (of Coriolanus, for instance,
sparing Rome at the entreaty of his wife and daughter).
In the historical age Cornelia moulded her sons the
Gracchi; Marius' wife accompanied him on his campaign against the Teutons; Metella influenced her husband Sulla; Lucullus had to sue through Cethegus'
mistress Praecia for the command against Mithridates.
Through dynastic marriages women were the cement
of political parties. Their influence owed something to
the precedent of the Hellenistic Queens. The death of
so many men in the civil wars increased their power.
Sallust alleged that a leading spirit among the
Catilinarian conspirators was the cultivated, ac-
complished, witty Sempronia. We catch a direct
glimpse in a letter Cicero wrote to Atticus three

months after the assassination of Caesar: 'I got to Antium on the 8th. Brutus was delighted to see me. Then, in front of Servilia, Tertia and Portia he asked me my opinion of the situation.' (These were Brutus' mother, half-sister, and wife.) Servilia in particular, who had once been Caesar's mistress, takes part in the subsequent discussion, even undertaking to get a clause deleted from a Senatorial bill. Four years later we find Antony's wife Fulvia raising legions and actually commanding them in the field. Livia's influence with Augustus was more discreet, but all the weightier because his power was absolute; and it was notorious that Claudius was dominated by his wives Messalina and Agrippina. But though imperial women would receive the highest honours, including posthumous deification, no one ever suggested that there should be an Empress Regnant of Rome.

Legally, however, all Roman women had a guardian, called *tutor*, like the Greek *kyrios;* Cicero said it was because of their weakness in judgment. This was the male head of the family, the *paterfamilias*, who, under the form of marriage that became usual, was not superseded by the husband when she married. He could not only decide whom she should marry, but could subsequently dissolve the marriage. (A signal instance occurred when, for dynastic reasons, Augustus compelled his stepson Tiberius to divorce a much-loved wife and marry his own recently widowed daughter Julia.) In Rome also the double standard of sexual morality was traditional. A wife had to remain faithful under threat of dire penalties, whereas a husband could with impunity indulge himself elsewhere provided he abstained from the wives and daughters of citizens. When the killing of many intestate men and their sons in the Hannibalic Wars had resulted in the enrichment of daughters, the receipt of legacies by women of the richest ratings was forbidden by a law of 169 BC. All this may seem intolerable. But in practice the restrictions melted with time. The longer a wife was away from the parental roof, and the oftener and further her husband was away on campaigns, the more independent she became. The Spartan experience was repeated. Legal fictions were evolved by which, if her *paterfamilias* died, she could substitute for whoever was left as her guardian someone of her own choosing. The Augustan 'three-children rights' included exemption from having a guardian. And as for the penalties for adultery they do not seem to have worried women like Clodia (the villainess of Cicero's speech *Pro Caelio*) who was in all probability the promiscuous Lesbia of Catullus.

Already at the beginning of the second century women had won a significant social victory. In the first crisis of the Hannibalic War the men had passed a law forbidding them to own more than half an ounce of gold, to wear multi-coloured dresses, or to ride in a two-horsed vehicle in the city. Six years after the war was over they demonstrated *en masse* for its repeal, lobbied magistrates on their way to the Forum, blockaded two tribunes in their houses, and succeeded despite bitter opposition from Cato, who is said to have complained, 'All peoples rule their wives; we rule all peoples; *our* wives rule us.'

The Romans were conscious indeed that their women had more social freedom than those of the

Greeks. Being generally richer, they could leave more household duties to slaves. A girl received primary education with the boys, and was often taught singing and dancing of a reputable kind. She might receive higher education from her mother or some gifted slave; and bluestockings were not uncommon. Cultural accomplishments were considered an enhancement. As a wife, as soon as she crossed her husband's threshold, usually at the age of twelve to fifteen if it was her first marriage, she was addressed by the household as *domina*. She lived, not in secluded quarters, but in the hall, where she received callers. She helped to issue invitations, and dined with her husband, at home or elsewhere, whoever was present. If she went out, she either walked with an attendant or was carried in a litter. In either case men made way for her, even the consul and his lictors. She gave her mouth to kiss to relations as far removed as second cousins. Only the cynical would agree with Cato that this was a breathalyser test designed by men to deter her from drinking.[5]

The six vestal virgins were in a peculiar position. They could not marry during the thirty years of their religious dedication, and the penalty for unchastity was burial alive, an effective deterrent to candidature. On the other hand, they were freed from guardianship and

[5] It is true however that the Romans were concerned about this. Excessive drinking by a wife could be grounds for divorce; and in repaying the dowry of a wife he was divorcing a husband could make a deduction on the score of her having drunk 'more than health required'. It has been suggested that the worry was, not that wine might inflame lust and so lead to adultery, but that it was believed to have contraceptive and abortifacient properties.

other legal restrictions applied to women. They also had privileges denied to all but men of high status—the right to drive through Rome in a gig, to be preceded by a lictor, and to sit in the best seats in the theatre.

We have one unique relic that brings us directly into touch with a girl born and reared in the highest society at the time of the transition from Republic to Principate, the half-dozen short poems (only forty lines in all) of Sulpicia, granddaughter of Cicero's friend, the great jurist Servius Sulpicius. With reckless freedom she speaks out about her love for a young man she calls Cerinthus. Her impulsive use of language can obscure her meaning, but here is a bare rendering of the poem that marks the apex of the affair:

> At last has come such a love, that I should be no less ashamed to cloak it than to lay it bare to another: the goddess of Cythera, yielding to my Muses, has brought him and laid him in my arms. Venus has fulfilled her promise: anyone who has had no joys of her own may tell of mine. I have no wish to seal up what I write for fear someone should read it sooner than my loved one. No, I glory in my offence, and am sick of tempering my face to reputation. Let it be said that we were a pair worthy of each other.

It would seem that women citizens in the late Roman Republic had a less inhibited life than any such class until quite modern times. I say 'the late Republic' because soon after that the conviction that liberty had become licence led Augustus to introduce legislation regulating sexual and matrimonial matters. While this still did nothing to penalise a husband who was unfaithful provided it was not with the daughter or wife of a

73

Roman citizen, or with a male citizen, it transferred adultery from the family tribunal, where partiality might result in leniency, to a new public tribunal, where the standard penalty for the woman was banishment to an island with the loss of half her dowry and a third of her other property. There was bitter opposition to this legislation, and at least until Vespasian's time it was not very effective. But things were never quite the same again.

Some high-born women escaped by registering as prostitutes, but Tiberius put a stop to that. It would be a mistake, however, to assume that the whole community followed the behaviour of high society. Numerous inscriptions, corresponding to those funeral monuments in Athens, such as the famous 'Praise of Turia', make it clear that a high conception of marriage continued to gain ground in the Greco-Roman world. There were signal instances of wifely devotion in the perils of the civil wars.

Plutarch touches essentials when he says that physical union with a wife initiates a love that resembles communion in the Great Mysteries; for sexual mutuality in marriage is something that deeply concerns women's liberation. We saw the demarcation made by that Athenian orator, relegating marital intercourse to the sole purpose of breeding. The ancients, unlike many moderns, were fully conscious of women's sexuality. Indeed, they thought it was keener than that of men. There was a legend of Zeus and Hera in relaxed mood, arguing as to which had most pleasure in sexual intercourse, male or female. Tiresias was summoned, as being the only possible adjudicator, having been both in his day. His verdict was: women, nine times as much. Aristotle did not want girls to marry too young partly because they would be too demanding sexually. Wives were expected to moderate their demands. This idea was deeply rooted at Rome also: intercourse in marriage was not for pleasure. Seneca (anticipating Mary Wollstonecraft) says, 'Nothing is more digusting than to love one's wife as though she were a mistress . . .' And Lucretius, in a well-known passage, anticipates the Victorian principle that 'Ladies don't move'.

The sexual deprivation thus caused to many women should not be underestimated; nor should the pain caused to them by the licence given to husbands to indulge in extra-marital amours. The archetypal wife was Hera, limited herself to Zeus's bed but continually hurt and humiliated by his roving amours. And indeed the whole ancient attitude to marriage was by decent modern standards an outrage to women's feelings.

A girl in her early teens is betrothed, for family reasons, to someone considerably older than herself whom she may even never have seen before. Plutarch realised that fear would be the dominant emotion of many a tender bride. Women were pushed about. The only mitigation was that divorce was easy, both in Greece and Rome, and in a marriage subsequent to the first a woman might have more choice. Augustus penalised any childless widow aged twenty to fifty who did not marry again within two years. The way in which high-born women were used as counters in the eugenic, social, and political game is astonishing.

The story of the orator Hortensius is a sufficient example. Wishing to ally himself to that paragon of virtue, the younger Cato, he asked if he could marry his wife, who had borne him three children. Cato agreed, so long as her father consented. We are not told what *she* said; the deal took place. On Hortensius' death Cato remarried the wife, now considerably richer. It is hard to believe that the wives were always, or even often, willing accomplices in such transactions, that they did not find some of the men into whose beds they were shunted positively repellent. And there is one corollary that is hardly ever mentioned, as if it didn't matter: the children of divorced parents (in Greece, probably, and in Rome, one is left to assume) went with the father. But that did not mean that a mother would forget her child. Thirty-seven years after her divorce from Augustus Scribonia voluntarily joined their daughter Julia in exile.

Occasionally the veil is lifted: the wrongs of women were eloquently expressed by Euripides in the mouth of his Medea:

Of all things that have life and understanding we women are the most unhappy creatures. First, we must buy a husband for a great sum, and take a master for our bodies, which is an even greater evil. And this is where we put most at stake: we may get a good husband or a bad. For women cannot be divorced without losing their good name, neither can they refuse a husband . . . But a husband, if he finds his home awkward, can relieve his tedium elsewhere, while we must depend on a single being. They say of us that we pass our lives safely at home,

while the men go out to battle. That shows their lack
of judgement. I would sooner fight three battles than
bear one child.[6]

There were always, of course, the consolations of
religion. At Athens a woman could be initiated into the
Eleusinian Mysteries. Lysias, in love with a *hetaera*,
had her initiated: this, if nothing else, he said, her
'madam' Nicarete could not take from her. The particular susceptibility of women to religious enthusiasm
was recognised in the institution of the Bacchic rites.
These, when introduced into Italy, led to the great
scandal of 186 BC and subsequent repression. But the
quieter religion of Isis had an increasing number of
women devotees as time went on, though perhaps
more among the humbler members of society than the
great Roman matrons involved in the state and family
cults. 'You gave women equal power with men', says
one of her hymns.

Christianity welcomed women, but as regards freedom
and equality with men in this life they were sent back to
square one. In the *First Epistle to Timothy* (New
English Bible version) we read:

Women must dress in a becoming manner, modestly
and soberly, not decked out with gold or pearls, or
expensive clothes, but with good deeds, as befits
women who claim to be religious. A woman must be
a learner, listening quietly and with due submission.

[6] Plato and Aristotle agreed with these sentiments, and later the
Stoics. The point is also made eloquently by the old woman slave
Syra in Plautus' *Mercator* (817–29), a play based on a Greek one of
the fourth century by Philemon.

I do not permit a woman to be a teacher, nor must woman domineer over man; she should be quiet. For Adam was created first, and Eve afterwards, and it was not Adam who was deceived; it was the woman who, yielding to deception, fell into sin. Yet she will be saved through motherhood—if only women continue in faith, love and holiness, with a sober mind.

Thus did the Hebrew story of Adam and Eve help to undo the liberalising process of centuries in the Greco-Roman world, and a pattern became established for women in Christendom which has persisted down to the twentieth century.

To sum up: there were no doubt plenty of wives who were perfectly contented with their lot, but who would be anathema to the modern enemies of male complacency. Such a one was the younger Pliny's wife who (he tells us) acquired an interest in literature to please him; learned his forensic speeches by heart and was all agog to hear how they had gone down; listened behind a curtain when he recited in the hope of overhearing compliments to retail to him; and set his poems to music with no teacher save love. But, for an approach to the independence modern feminists seek, we must think of a Spartiate wife of the early fourth century; or a *grande cocotte* of that century hitched up to some wealthy and influential man; or a willing drop-out like the Cynic Hipparchia; or a quiet enjoyer of the garden of Epicurus; or a physician in Hellenistic Greece; or a society woman in the late Roman Republic.

THREE

III

Nudism in Deed and Word

LET me first define and clarify. By 'nudism in deed' I mean a wilful overcoming of the taboos which have established themselves among civilised people against exposing certain parts of the body. Of course primitive man went naked, and remains so in some parts of the world: and some tribes are coy about parts we are not ashamed of exposing yet surprised at what missionaries bid them conceal. To others obscenity would be a meaningless conception. But by 'nudism' I mean a display of total nakedness, including the genital zones, to which among civilised peoples the feeling of shame is primarily attached. How fundamental this feeling of shame is, the Book of Genesis testifies: for the Jews it was the first element of human sensibility that seemed to demand an aetiological myth. By 'nudism in word' I mean the wilful overcoming of the corresponding taboo which early led to the use of euphemisms about the genital organs and their functions.

The two kinds of 'nudism' are not unconnected. Besides concerning the same field of ideas, they often have a common motivation, exhibitionism and a desire to shock. Quintilian actually uses the phrase 'naked words'. But when nudism re-emerges, whether in life or art, among people who have left primitive nakedness far behind them we should not assume a single common motive, any more than for the origin of clothing. There are such things for instance, as religious nudism and religious obscenity.

In modern times there have been sporadic outcrops of nudism, whether on Scandinavian beaches, or in suburban societies (which have generally been regarded as cranky but not orgiastic), or among dissident communities such as the immigrant Dukhobors in western Canada. After the Russian Revolution some of the young expressed their sense of liberation by nudism, which shocked the Old Bolsheviks. But what makes the subject topical—even if we disregard 'streaking', which appears to have been a transient prank, and the extension to 'pop' festivals of the previously secluded nudism of societies—is the recent invasion of the world of entertainment by full frontal nudity. It is only a few years since newspapers gave headlines to the brief appearance in this state of an actress in a Swedish film.[1] Next came *Hair* (1968) and *Oh Calcutta!* (1969), nude Dutch ballet dancers, and a Desdemona strangled in the nude in defiance of Shakespeare's intentions. Some call this exploration, other exploitation. More important for my particular purpose was the appearance of Lord Clark's admirable book *The Nude: A Study of Ideal Art* (John Murray 1956); for it was the Greeks who, by their adoption of nudity in athletics and elevation of it in art, made the most significant contribution to our subject.

[1] As to films the process is traced step by step by John Trevelyan, in *What the Censor Saw* (1973).

Complete nudity is very rare in ancient Sumerian, Assyrian, Babylonian and Egyptian art. It is almost confined to captives, on whom it was inflicted as a degradation. This idea of degradation occurs also in Homer. Odysseus threatens to teach Thersites his place by stripping from him the garments that cover his 'shame' (*aidos*); and the body of Hector that Achilles drags behind his chariot round the walls of Troy is naked.[2] Of course the nakedness of captives might be simply the result of despoliation; but the idea that nakedness could be cause for mockery persists, being attributed, for instance, to barbarians by Plato. On the other hand religious nakedness was not uncommon. It plays a part in initiation ceremonies. People praying or processing are represented as naked. So are mourners. On vases of the early so-called Geometric period women parade naked before the dead. Alexander the Great and his friends processed naked round the tomb of Achilles as a mark of homage. In some societies women expose themselves to the sky to attract rain; in others prophets and prophetesses bare themselves to inspiration. On the other hand nakedness can be apotropaic, to ward off danger. We need not speculate here on the ideas that lay behind such customs; but what seems clear is that nakedness was felt to be something of special significance.

As to our perception of Greek custom, there is a terminological difficulty that obfuscates the evidence, in that the word *gymnos*, which normally means naked, *can* be used to mean lightly clad. But it is much too often assumed to mean the latter by translators

[2] A millennium later Tigranes, King of Armenia, submitted himself naked to the mercy of Pompey.

who cannot divest themselves of our preconceptions.

Works of art show that in Minoan-Mycenean times even acrobats and others engaging in physical exercise wore at least a kind of tight-fitting shorts. In Homer heroes strip to sleep, but in public show the same modesty as most moderns. Odysseus, emerging from the bushes after his shipwreck to accost Nausicaa, holds a branch before him to hide his nakedness; and he asks her and her companions to withdraw while he washes in a stream. He is careful also not to strip wholly naked for his wrestling-match with Irus. It is true that when a hero took a bath handmaids assisted, but that can happen to anyone today in Helsinki or Tokyo. The only thing that strikes us as strange is when a guest is bathed and anointed by his hostess, as Telemachus is by Nestor's younger daughter, and Odysseus by Circe, even indeed by Helen when he came disguised into Troy.

From early times, however, there was one feature of the Greek scene, a feature which persisted into the classical period, that has always struck modern people as incongruous in what was in so many ways a highly civilised culture; the ubiquity of phallic symbols, magic promoters of fertility. Enormous and astonishing ones lined the Sacred Way at Delos, and were carried in Dionysiac processions. The leather ones worn by the actors in Attic Comedy could be, of course, the subject of jokes; but in origin they were serious adjuncts to the rites of Dionysus. Nor had phalli lost their religious significance for the commons of Athens even in Aristophanes' time—as can be deduced from the superstitious dismay that took hold of these when, just before the Sicilian Expedition was to set sail, they awoke to find that in the night the Herms, the square pedestals surmounted by busts of deities which were a common sight in the streets and squares of the city, had been mutilated. To some extent, therefore, both sexes were accustomed to sights which to us would be more shocking even than male nakedness in public.

There are various accounts of how nudity invaded Greek athletics.

It would seem that something revolutionary occurred at the 15th Olympic Games in 750 BC. Thucydides however asserts that it was introduced 'quite recently'; Plato a generation later says the same. The former attributes it to Spartans, the latter to Cretans followed by Spartans—Dorians in either case. It has been noted that in art the prevalence of nudity characterises Greeks of the peninsula and Cyclades rather than those of Asia Minor and its offshore islands; and as for barbarians, Herodotus remarks that among them it is shameful even for a man to be seen naked, implying that for Greeks it was a commonplace. There is some doubt as to when nakedness was introduced for running, in which it would actually be a disadvantage, and how consistently it was maintained before the fifth century; but at least it seems to have been adopted early and permanently for boxing and wrestling.[3] In any case, however, what matters is not how or when the break-

---

[3] E. N. Gardiner points to two black-figured vases on which runners are portrayed wearing jockstraps; but in the wrestling-school at least nudity was practically invariable in the sixth century, to judge from vase-paintings. The great age of Spartan athletics was 720–576 BC.

through took place, but the fact that it did, and that nudity in athletics and gymnastics was a peculiarity to Greeks of which they became proud. Even older men continued to exercise naked. Male spectators were admitted to gymnasia and wrestling-schools as well as to athletic contests, but not females. At the Olympic Games, by one account, no woman might cross the River Alpheus for a stated number of days (though Pausanias says that unmarried girls could watch, and a seat was reserved for the priestess of Demeter). Women had their own games there at another time, the *Heraea,* in which unmarried girls ran in short tunics with their right shoulder bare.

The exercises made young men proud of their bodies, exposed as they were for a large part of the day, and ashamed not to keep them in the best possible condition; and until professionalism in the Hellenistic Age led to muscular over-development of certain parts, they attained a high standard of harmonious beauty. Greeks acquired an intense appreciation of the male human body, as a whole, observed in all sorts of poses. Chaerophon exclaims in Plato's *Charmides*:

> What a handsome face he has; but if he were naked you would forget he had a face, he is so beautiful in every way.[4]

Of course there was an element of the erotic in this appreciation. The statues in gymnasia usually included one of Eros; and it can be no accident that the heyday of Greek amateur athletics coincided with that of homosexual love, which prevailed in precisely those parts

[4] Everyone gazed at him 'as though he were a statue', a phrase that would hardly occur to a modern writer.

of the Hellenic world that were most given to these pursuits. But the body can express other intense human emotions also, and body and spirit were felt as one.

There was however, an even stronger element of idealisation, a pride in nudity, a feeling that there was in it something heroic and indeed divine. The Games themselves, we must remember, were religious festivals. This feeling about divinity and the male nude was progressively concentrated in the worship of Apollo.

Appreciation of the male human body found expression, especially at Athens, in art. Male nudes had been common on the Dipylon vases of the eighth century, though as yet highly schematised. In the seventh century they became established as the proper subject of fine art, hence the series of statues of youths called *kouroi*. Adulation of successful athletes, heroes on earth, led to the commissioning of statues of them. In these the body was not neglected at the expense of the head, a fact emphasised by the rarity of busts in the classical period. Intent observation produced a gradual progression in naturalism, culminating in a sudden leap forward about 480 BC, in the great days of the repulse of the Persians, which produced the marble youth of Critios on the Acropolis. But it was, in sculpture at least, an idealised naturalism, behind which lie perceptions, and apparently actual canons, of harmonious proportion, whose inspiration comes from a mathematical aesthetic sense as much as from the actualities of human bodies. In the words of Kenneth Clark:

What both Reynolds and Blake meant by ideal beauty was really the diffused memory of that

peculiar physical type which was developed in
Greece between 480 and 440 BC, and which, in vary-
ing degrees of intensity and consciousness, furnished
the mind of Western man with a pattern of perfection
from the Renaissance to the present century.[5]

These statues were of *young* men only. The Greeks
felt strongly the difference between exposure in the
young and the older. Thus the early Spartan poet Tyr-
taeus, after exclaiming what an ugly and shameful sight
it is to see an elder, wounded in battle, with his flesh
laid bare, grasping his bloodied privates in both hands,
immediately adds, 'but in the young anything is
seemly'. Similarly, for statues of older males some
drapery was generally considered proper. The young
male nude remained the favourite subject of sculptors,
and new formulations continued to be made right
down to late Hellenistic times.

The question arises, how far does nudity in Greek art
reflect nudity in real life? When art re-emerges after the
long Dark Age and human figures eventually appear on
the so-called Geometric pottery of the eighth century,
men are often (and women quite often) depicted as
naked. The figures are however highly schematised;
and in some cases it is difficult to tell the sexes apart,
though women may be distinguished by token triangu-
lar projections for breasts and later by hatched skirts.
The treatment was conceptual rather than realistic. It
does appear, however, that nakedness in women is
associated in the paintings with religion and

[6] *The Nude, II.*

mourning, and occasionally with strenuous indoor work such as spinning and weaving; and on one and the same vase they may be shown as naked in one context, clothed in another. To this extent conformity with life may have been a guiding principle.

The nudity that occurs in seventh and sixth century vases seems discontinuous from the Geometric tradition. It is related not only to the introduction of athletic nudity, but to the development of technique that substituted for abstract design representational painting which was always seeking more perfect naturalism. Humanity has become the centre of interest. But we still have to ask: How far does art mirror real life? Thus warriors are sometimes represented as exposed in the parts below their cuirass. Exposure for either magic, i.e. apotropaic, purposes or alternatively for psychological shock effect, is not unknown among primitive warriors. It is conceivable that even in seventh- and sixth-century Greece some men fought in this guise, without the undertunic worn in Homeric times, though it seems unlikely. But when it comes to warriors depicted as fighting in only a helmet and shield, or to legendary heroes grappling naked with enemies, it is clear that artistic idealisation has taken over.

Women, on the other hand, rarely appear naked on vases of this period except within certain limits. The exceptions include scenes from mythology where it would be appropriate, as in the case of Atalanta, or scenes, from Bacchic revels (though often the Maenads are fully clad), and erotic scenes of nymphs and satyrs. For the rest, women are sometimes shown as naked at the bath. But above all they appear naked in dances, routs, and men's drinking parties, engaged in what is now known as group sex, or playing the flute; and here we may be sure they are *hetaerae*. It would seem that mythology offered a convenient excuse for licentious fancy, but that otherwise the paintings reflect distinctions that existed in real life. This fashion began with the wine-cups produced from about 530 BC and lasted some fifty years. It was always strongest on the Greek mainland, becoming weaker progressively towards the east, among the Ionians sensitive to Persian influence.

What is less clear is, how typical the vase-paintings are. In the first place, artistic fashions easily establish themselves, so that one kind of subject matter not at all typical of ordinary life may loom unduly large. Also, for our present purpose, the overall conspectus may be distorted by the fact that from the sixth century, as artists became more competent in the naturalistic rendering of the human form, there developed a considerable industry in what we should call pornographic art, emanating particularly from Corinth, the erotic capital of Greece. You could justify anything by giving a man engaged in erotic activity a horse's tail and calling him a satyr.

The extent of this industry is very hard to estimate, because museums have hidden away so many specimens in their cellars; and the producers of books on vase-painting have tended to include only an occasional example, at most, among their illustrations. It can only be even roughly judged by someone who has the opportunity and the industry to plough through the fascicules, amounting to a hundred or so, of the

Corpus Vasorum Antiquorum. Of course not all the love scenes depicted deserve to be classed as pornographic; they can be tender and moving, in accordance with what was best in the Greek spirit.

Vases were an intimate form of art. In fullsized sculpture, designed as it was mainly for public display, we have, even from as late as the fifth century, scarcely any female nudes. The earliest is the so-called Esquiline Venus. She is, incidentally, mathematically proportioned, but not as a close copy of a model would be (the head-length being taken as the unit, she is seven heads tall, one head separates her breasts, one her breasts and navel, and one her navel and crotch). Another is the flute-girl on the side of the so-called Ludovisi Throne, also now at Rome. On this the central figure rising on the front panel between two attendants is draped. She is commonly taken to be Aphrodite rising from the sea; and it is a remarkable fact that until the fourth century even the goddess of love is nearly always represented, by contrast with Apollo, as draped. One remembers the legends of Actaeon and Tiresias, respectively torn by hounds and blinded, for even accidentally seeing a goddess naked.

Transparent draperies for women appear in Phidias' work and we have a nude Aphrodite in a late fifth-century bronze. (We must not forget that marble statues we know may have had predecessors—bronzes long since melted down and large-scale paintings long since lost.) But what seems to have made the breakthrough for the female nude in sculpture was the fourth-century vogue for the *grandes cocottes*, who were proud to model for statues of Aphrodite.

Aphrodite succeeded Apollo as the favourite deity of the age. It was Praxiteles who established the classic female nude. Even so, the idea that Aphrodite should be draped died hard. While Praxiteles made for the Cnidians a nude statue of her modelled on the courtesan Cratine,[6] which was to become the most famous statue of antiquity, he made a draped one for the Coans. (The Cnidian Aphrodite, incidentally, has the same proportions as the Esquiline Venus.)

In these nudes, as in those of males, the Greek idealising tendency is strongly expressed. We find it as early as in the dying Niobid of about 450 BC in the Museo delle Terme at Rome, whose dress is slipping off so that she is virtually nude. Aristotle was to find a way of describing what the idealising artist does in terms of his own philosophy: 'The artist gives us knowledge of Nature's unrealised aims.' This development was not merely aesthetic: it reflected the new interest in women of the Age of Enlightenment.

At a meeting of the Archaeological Institute in London (on June 8, 1877) Madame Sophia Schliemann gave an address on the contribution of Greece to civilisation. When she had finished, Heinrich Schliemann rose and asked permission to add something, and it was this:

Another of the agents instrumental in producing a high perfection of art in ancient Greece was the entire absence of our present code of conventional proprieties and the perfect freedom which the fair

[6] Probably her and not, as another tradition had it, the more famous Phryne, of whom a nude statue in bronze was dedicated at Delphi.

sex enjoyed regarding dress, which was consequently in analogy to the hot climate and hardly
amounted to anything at all.

'(A laugh)' *The Times* account reports in brackets.

'Being thus all his life', continued Schliemann unde-
terred, 'surrounded with masterpieces of nature, the
ancient Greek artist was at liberty constantly to study
the symmetry and anatomy of the female body, and he
could produce wonders by merely copying what he
saw.' Mr Gladstone, billed to speak next, felt con-
strained to disagree. 'The nation at large', he said, 'were
very decorously clad: their persons were wholly
covered. The exception, which proved the rule, was
Sparta, the least Greek of all Hellas in the fine feeling
for art.'

Now, in the first place, to what extent *was* Sparta an
exception as to female nudity in everyday life? Our
evidence is conflicting. Plutarch, writing in the second
century AD, says that Lycurgus encouraged the girls
there to go naked (*gymnos*) in processions and when
dancing and singing at certain festivals, in the presence
and under the eyes of the youths. Nor, he adds, was
there anything disgraceful in these strippings (*apodyseis*)
of maidens, since modesty attended them and inconti-
nence was banished; and they produced in them rather
habits of simplicity and an ardent desire for physical
well-being. Moreover, he says, there were in these customs incentives to marriage; for the youths were
attracted by a force which was, in Plato's words, not
dynamic but erotic. Such language implies, though not
inescapably, that complete nudity was involved, and
Roman writers certainly assumed that this was the case.

It may, however, depend on what period of time is in question, for as to the fifth century BC we have striking evidence to the contrary in Euripides. In his *Andromache* Peleus inveighs against Spartan women for shamelessness in going out to exercise among men with thighs bared and dress girt up. If they had been completely naked, *a fortiori* he would surely have said so; and there exist also Spartan statuettes from the sixth and fifth centuries of girls running in short skirts. Further, a scholiast on Euripides' *Hecuba* says that they were dressed in a single skirt (*monochitones*) in their athletic contests. So it seems likely that, in this period at least, they wore something rather less scanty than they do, for instance, in Degas' famous picture in the National Gallery, *Girls in ancient Sparta inciting the boys to wrestle*. Nor, for that matter, need we suppose that they wrestled *with* boys rather than with each other in the company of boys. It may also be relevant that Plato in the *Laws*, a work which borrows much from Spartan customs, prescribes that only girls below the age of puberty shall race naked: those aged thirteen and over must be suitably clad. Likewise, when he proposes that before marriages are fixed up, in order that prospective husbands and fathers-in-law should have close personal knowledge of eligible girls, sportive mixed dances should be arranged, he stipulates that both youths and girls should be unclad only as far as modesty permits in either case.

As to the rest of Greece, Schliemann was of course wildly mistaken, whereas Gladstone only failed to recall the peculiar athletic and gymnastic nudity of males. Dorian women were not so very scantily clothed in their *peplos*, and Ionian ones were draped from head to foot in their *chiton* with its many folds. Nor did women parade themselves in public. The archaic Athenian statues of women called *korai* are fundamentally male *kouroi* with genitals suppressed, small breasts added, the clinging draperies superimposed. Artists had few opportunities in everyday life of studying women's bodies as they studied men's in the gymnasia.[7] Though prostitutes might no doubt have been hired to pose, this seems not to have been done in the archaic and early classical periods. What artists were successful in representing was what they could observe in everyday life.

Not but what it seems probable that *hetaerae* or slave girls appeared in the nude as mute characters on the comic stage. This has been hotly denied, but also maintained by distinguished scholars from Wilamowitz to the present day. At least two jokes in Aristophanes are inexplicable otherwise—unless one prefers to believe that the parts were played by males in flesh-coloured tights realistically painted. There are several other places in his comedies where female nudes are introduced and attention is drawn to their attractions. Sometimes the introducion is gratuitous, and would have little justification in the audience's eyes unless it really did display an attractive woman—though here the nudity can be no more than plausibly alleged on the analogy of the two cases I have mentioned.
The younger and more adventurous Plato of the

[7] Though more perhaps than the boy H. G. Wells, whose first erotic fantasies, in an age of flounces and crinolines, were perforce inspired by the nearest thing he had ever seen to the latent female form, the symbolic figures of Britannia, Erin, etc. in Tenniel's *Punch* cartoons.

Republic, having decided on principle that women should be eligible as guardians just as much as men, followed this to its logical conclusion:

> Many of the things we are talking about would seem absurdly unconventional if they were put into practice. The most absurd sight—don't you think?—would be women stripping with the men in the wrestling schools, and not only the young ones, but even the older ones, as happens in our gymnasia where men continue to cultivate gymnastics even when they are wrinkled and no longer pleasant to look at.

Plato is at pains to urge that one must not be deterred by ridicule from putting principles into effect. Male nudity in the gymnasium (he alleges) was quite a recent innovation, and though wags may have laughed at it at first, now only barbarians did: the same might prove to be the case with female nudity.

Another defence of nudism on principle was produced in this same fourth century, by the Cynic sect. Holding that life should be lived according to nature, they challenged all conventions. One of the corollaries was a cult of shamelessness (*anaideia*). Diogenes is reported to have performed sexual acts in public; and he too thought that women should exercise along with men. Zeno, the founder of Stoicism, inherited this defiance of shame. 'What is natural cannot be disgraceful'—in the familiar Latin formulation, *naturalia non sunt turpia*; and nakedness was adjudged more natural than shame. But how far such doctrinaire teaching affected the conduct of people at large in the Hellenistic Age is hard to determine.

The Romans' attitude to nudity was originally that of most barbarians. It was degrading for a citizen to be seen naked. Cicero quotes with approval a line from Ennius to the effect that stripping among citizens is the origin of vice; and he attributes the same view to the younger Scipio. Competitive athletics and gymnastics were a spectacle, something put on by professionals, not a way of life for citizens, and such indeed they had become in contemporary Greece. People had their slaves trained as athletes. And even under the Empire, when Roman citizens had begun to compete, complete nudity was long excluded; so that Tacitus could say in disapproval of Nero's inauguration of games, 'The next step will be that people will be compelled to strip naked.' Boys did wrestle, however, and Seneca deplores people who sat and watched them: 'For we are beset by vices that are not even Roman. What a scandal!'

Nero encouraged adult Romans to wrestle and box, but in Domitian's Capitoline Games competition was left mainly to Greek athletes. We know of only one Roman citizen in the first century AD who appeared in the stadium. The native Roman spectacles were military exercises such as the equestrian Troy Game, reintroduced by Augustus and described in Virgil's Fifth Aeneid. Young men did practise field sports, such as discus- and javelin-throwing, and ball games, in the Campus Martius, but not in the nude, so far as we know.

As to art, the influx of Greek statues that began in the third century BC accustomed the Romans to nudity, especially in those of the gods. Greek works of art were copied, as in the beautiful female nude painted on a wall in the House of the Mysteries at Pompeii. Portrait heads of deified emperors were placed, with tasteless incongruity, on idealised nude bodies slavishly imitated from statues of gods of the great Greek period. The result is as embarrassing as Canova's nude Napoleon. But the true Roman statue was always of a man in toga or armour. There was, however, one notable exception: Hadrian's favourite Antinoüs. After his death there was a proliferation of portrait statues and busts of him, about five hundred of which survive, mostly copies of ones made from the life. These include the only important nudes produced under Rome (the nudity denoted deification). It would seem that his mysterious, melancholy grace inspired some artist or artists with a direct apperception of male beauty unknown for centuries; and, again in the words of Kenneth Clark, 'The physical character of Antinoüs is still perceptible when, after its long banishment, the Apollonian nude returns in the person of Donatello's David. ...'[8]

On the stage, Roman actors, who were all males except in the mime, wore a sort of loincloth or jockstrap called *subligar* or *subligaculum* as a precaution against involuntary exposure. There was one exceptional occasion, the annual festival of the Floralia, no doubt originally a fertility festival. At this the performances were by women prostitutes, and obscenity was the order of the day. As a culmination they stripped at the bidding of the audience. There is a story that on one occasion the people held back from this because of the presence of that paragon of virtue, the younger Cato; but at a hint from a friend he tactfully withdrew so

[8] *The Nude*, 44.

as not to spoil the fun. There also became popular in the Greek part of the Roman world what was known as the Pyrrhic Dance, a representation, sometimes by well-born young people, of mythological subjects. Apuleius describes one at Corinth, a Judgment of Paris in which Mercury, a beautiful youth, wore only a cloak, and Venus only a transparent drapery which a breath of wind wafted aside. Off the stage, too, 'see-through' clothes, generally of Coan silk, became fashionable by Augustan times in permissive circles, and are duly deprecated by moralists. Later the Christians in particular denounced all forms of nude exhibition, including the Floralia and the erotic nudity which had by then become common in the theatrical and aquatic spectacles of the Empire.

But if the Romans 'in their most high and palmy days' rejected the nudity of Greek athletics as corrupting, they made up for this by developing far more than the Greeks the institution of warm and cold indoor baths, which the Greeks considered suitable mainly for the sick and aged, but which had thoroughly taken hold of all classes in Italy by the end of the Republic. The baths, with their recreational and cultural facilities, became for the Romans a way of life, as the gymnasia had become for the Greeks. In these the wearing of a *subligar* was optional, at least for males, and probably exceptional. Young men also plunged into the Tiber after exercising in the Campus Martius. Cicero accuses Clodia of acquiring gardens on the river bank opposite for the purpose of making assignations with bathers. But whether or not they wore anything, we are not told.

In early times, and later too in less opulent towns, men and women bathed at different hours. But separate baths, or sections of baths, for women began to be introduced in the second century BC. Even upper class women such as Augustus' mother frequented them. Women wore a *subligar*, perhaps a bikini outfit like that of the ballplaying girls in the well-known mosaic at Piazza Armerina in Sicily, or even a larger bathing dress. The divinity Fortuna Virilis (Luck with Men) was worshipped, we are told, by the poorer class of women in the men's baths, because there those parts of the human body are uncovered which seek women's favour. (Her festival was on April 1.). In the general permissiveness of the Empire mixed bathing became more widely prevalent. It was forbidden by Hadrian, but ineffectively, as repeated prohibitions by later Emperors show. This does not mean that respectable matrons indulged in it. Quintilian, in fact, calls it the sort of thing adulteresses do; and it was another of the practices condemned by Christian writers.

A Roman father and son did not bathe together after the son attained puberty. This taboo of embarrassment is not peculiar to Romans, as the story of Noah and his sons in Genesis reminds us. But several ancient writers comment on the peculiarity that a Roman father-in-law and son-in-law also would not bathe together. Was this relationship felt to be unusually close? Catullus says surprisingly to his Lesbia, 'I loved you then not as the common man loves his mistress, but as a father loves his sons and sons-in-law.'

So much for the differences between Greece and Rome as to nudism in deed. One might sum up by saying that

100

in Greece, in the classical period, athletic nudism encouraged an appreciation of the young male form which was not without erotic undertones—unique, a source of pride, numinous and infinitely fruitful in the realm of art; whereas the Romans, from an instinctive and not abnormal recoil from Greek nudity and homosexuality, gradually relaxed their inhibitions, encouraged both by Hellenistic influence and by the eventual craze for public baths.

And now for 'nudism in word'. When Homer's Odysseus, threatening to strip Thersites, speaks of the garments that cover his 'shame', not his 'genitals', he is using a euphemism which shows that sexual words as well as sexual deeds were already a subject of taboos.

Naked words as well as naked deeds had their part in religion. There was a tradition that when the mourning Demeter came to Eleusis in her search for Persephone, she was cheered and made to laugh either by an obscene exposure or an obscene joke of a servant-girl. This was an aetiological myth for the fact that obscene acts and language were a feature of her festivals in historical times. No doubt the real reason was that these festivals originated in fertility rites. As L. R. Farnell says of the festival of the Thesmophoria at Athens:

> There was *aeschrologia*—badinage of an undoubtedly indecent kind . . . and this was no mere casual and licentious *jeu d'esprit* . . . but a conscientious duty steadily performed by matrons whose standard of chastity was probably as high as our own and ideas of refinement in other respects very like our own, the object of this, as of all the rest

of the ritual, being to stimulate the fertilising powers of the earth and the human frame.[9]

But euphemism was normal, as is shown by the use of 'the so-and-so' (*to deina*), or words such as 'foot' (*pous*), for the penis, and of 'the shameful things' (*aidoia*, in Latin *pudenda*), as the ordinary word for genitals. Aristotle rationalised verbal modesty:

> There is nothing [he writes in the *Politics*], that a legislator should be more careful to outlaw than indecency of speech; for the light utterance of shameful words soon leads to shameful actions. The young especially should never be allowed to hear or repeat anything of the sort.[10]

Aristophanes, of course, had notoriously used the frankest words; but that was no doubt to raise a laugh just because they were shocking. Aristotle notes however that while indecency of language was thought amusing in the Old Comedy of the fifth century (that of Aristophanes), the New Comedy of the fourth (that of Menander) relied rather on innuendo. And Plato the philosopher is particularly euphemistic. Aeschines, in his speech against Timarchus, apologises profusely to the jury for the words he is obliged to use as well as the subject he has to deal with. 'As for the offences and outrages that Pittalacus did to Timarchus, I would rather die than describe them to you in words.' This

[9] *The Cults of the Greek States*, Oxford, 1907, Vol. III, 104.
[10] Aristotle also wishes to banish obscene pictures, but makes the interesting exception of those in the temples of deities at whose festivals obscenity is in order.

suggests that words could shock ordinary citizens too.

But, like nudism in deed, nudism in word became involved in the controversy between the champions of nature and convention (*physis* and *nomos*). The primitive idea that a name is intimately connected with the person or thing that bears it was introduced into philosophy by Heraclitus, who held that language was natural in origin. Plato in his *Cratylus*, while supporting Heraclitus' theory in general, allowed for a considerable influence of convention.[11] But the Cynics believed that everything had its natural word, behind all the conventional euphemisms (metaphors, etc.), and that it was one's duty to use it in accordance with the principle of shamelessness. And this view was inherited by some of the Stoics.

Cicero wrote an interesting letter on this subject to his familiar friend Papirius Paetus, in reply to one in which Paetus had apparently referred to the penis by its natural name (*nomen proprium* or *nomen suum* in Latin) of '*mentula*'.[12] In it he summarises, with Latin illustrations substituted for the Greek, a defence by a cynicising Stoic of the thesis that there is no such thing as obscenity in deed or word. He cites scenes from a comedy and three tragedies which would be obscene if the matter were expressed in naked words, but which are felt to be unobjectionable because it is not. But,

[11] Plato did acknowledge the objection, obvious to us, that it was nature to barbarians to use words different from those of the Greeks.

[12] Cicero observes that the word penis itself (tail) is really a euphemism, but one which by frequent use has now come to seem just as obscene as the *nomen proprium*; but to Augustine 'penis' was still an unobjectionable term whereas 'the sordid and common word' would not be.

says the Stoic, actions in themselves, sexual intercourse, for instance, are not obscene; and if the thing or
action is not obscene, *a fortiori* the words describing it
cannot be. Again, why should certain innocent words
be avoided because they happen to have an alternative
obscene meaning? So the whole idea of obscenity is a
mare's nest, and the Stoic concludes, 'The wise man
will call a spade a spade!' But Cicero simply dismisses
the case out of hand, saying:

> I am glad that there is no word you feel you cannot
> use to me; but for my part I shall observe, and
> continue to observe (being so conditioned), the
> decency of Plato.

At the time when he wrote that letter Cicero was
studying Panaetius, the gentlemanly Stoic who had
been attached to the younger Scipio, for his *De Officiis*.
No doubt Panaetius dissented from the cynicising
branch; for Cicero here turns against it its own argument from Nature. Nature has tucked away the parts
of our body that are unsightly though necessary, and
human modesty has followed her; for all healthy-
minded people conceal those parts. Nor do they call
them or their functions by their real names. We should
not listen to the Cynics and Cynico-Stoics who taunt
us with inconsistency for thinking it disgraceful to
name some things which are not disgraceful to do,
while calling by their real names some things that are
so, such as robbery and fraud. Their whole philosophy
is an offence against decent feeling (*verecundia*), which
is an essential element of the right and honourable. Let
us rather follow Nature, Cicero says, and shun everything that offends our eyes or ears.

Cicero himself was not above obscene innuendo. Thus he could not resist taunting Clodius at a casual encounter with a punning allusion to his reputed incest with his sister, though he admits to Atticus that this joke may not have been in the best consular taste (*'parum consulare'*). But he does consistently deprecate obscene language, which he calls unworthy not only of the Forum but of the society of civilised people.[13] He warns orators against using words that have an alternative meaning which is obscene, and even against accidental collocations of syllables that would produce what sounded like an obscene word, with examples that throw an interesting light on Roman salacity (an increasing tendency to which Quintilian was to deplore); and he deprecates metaphors, however apt, that are obscene, such as calling Glaucia the ordure of the Senate house, or saying that by the death of Africanus the state had been castrated. The admired Stoic Posidonius had made a long list of acts so disgraceful that the wise man would not do them even to save his country. Cicero thought it unbecoming even to have mentioned some of them. The same line is taken by his admirer Quintilian. He is content with what he calls 'the old Roman custom of decency' (*Romanus pudor*). This he says he will maintain by observing silence on the subject; but that doesn't prevent him from giving shortly afterwards warning examples as astonishing as Cicero's of unintentional *double entendres* and collocations of syllables producing obscene words.

[13] In Petronius' *Satyricon* (132) Eumolpus addresses his penis, though as something unmentionable in any respectable context. Later he repents of having bandied words with a part of the body whose very existence men of stricter temper hardly admit.

The encyclopaedist Celsus, who wrote under Tiberius, expresses embarrassment when he comes, in his section on Medicine, to deal with genito-urinary diseases. He says that the names of the parts affected are more tolerable in their Greek forms, which often occur in medical writings and discourse; whereas Latin terms for obscene things have not become acceptable by usage, so that it is hard to deal with them with due regard for both decency and science. But he has decided that he should not be deterred by that, both so as not to omit any cure he has heard of and because it is particularly important to learn about the parts that people are least willing to show to each other. Thus when dealing with what the Greeks call *enterokele* and *epiplokele* he adds that Latin has a common but improper term, '*hernia*'.

It does seem that the Romans were as squeamish as we have traditionally been. They had various phrases of apology for calling a spade a spade.[14] For us 'the decent obscurity of a learned language' means Latin; for the Romans it meant Greek.

But there were recognised exceptions. In certain religious rites obscenity was of the essence. Thus at Lanuvium near Rome a whole month was dedicated to the Liberalia, the festival of the Italian equivalent of Bacchus. During it, citizens used the most disgraceful language, until finally the phallic symbol was carried round the market-place, wreathed by a matron, and

[14] One was '*honorem Kalendis Martiis*' ('with due respect for March 1'). March 1 was the feast of Matronalia, a day on which prudery would be particularly appropriate. Others were '*honorem praefari*', '*honos auribus sit*', and '*sit venia verbo*'.

put back in its repository. As to the language, this is the counterpart of the Athenian Thesmophoria. Again, in one of the old Roman marriage ceremonies there was a point at which obscene ribaldry was traditional—'Fescennine joking', it was called. In the otherwise exquisitely delicate prothalamium which Catullus composed for Manlius and Vinia this is represented by twitting the bridegroom with having a male concubine he will now have to give up. Here the obscenity was again no doubt originally aimed at the magical promotion of fertility; whereas in the ribald verses chanted by Roman soldiers at triumphs its original object may have been apotropaic, the warding off of envy.

Obscenity was also an essential ingredient of certain literary genres, the traditions of which were conscientiously observed. Catullus displays it in his invectives, using particularly shocking words to rebuke two acquaintances whom he represents as having inferred obscenity in his life from the obscenity of his verses. The brutally sadistic language of Horace's eighth and twelfth Epodes is in the tradition of the iambic genre as founded by Archilochus, and the frankness of satire is a legacy from its Roman founder Lucilius.

The history or permissiveness in twentieth-century Europe and America seems at first sight more parallel to the Roman than the Greek experience.

It is a revolt against the oppressive *mos maiorum*, the artificial restrictions and hypocrisies, of the nineteenth century. But it is also a crusade for freedom, for originality, for widening the bounds of spiritual experience, whose ultimate source is the French Revolution and the Romantic Movement, the generators of ideas such as those of Shelley and Godwin. In this it has more in common with the Greek movement that originated in Socrates' re-examination of accepted values and was carried to extremes by his avowed followers the Cynics, with their flouting of all conventions.

We see today the same mixture of libertarian propaganda and shocking for shocking's sake as characterised the Cynic behaviour and their diatribes or popular sermons. With us it is, still more, a form of (or substitute for) originality in the arts and literature. Of this whole movement nudism, whether in deed or word, is just one symptom.

FOUR

IV

Homosexuality

I WELL remember the slight *frisson* of surprise with which, some twenty-five years ago, I first read the word 'homosexuality' in the columns of *The Times* newspaper. It was then a subject hardly referred to in polite society or literature.

But in 1953 there occurred two or three court cases involving prominent people, and a converging movement gathered momentum, coming from the Howard League for Penal Reform, the Church of England Moral Welfare Council, initiatives of Sir Robert Boothby and Mr Desmond Donnelly in the House of Commons, the rebound of a hostile motion by Earl Winterton in the House of Lords, and certain newspapers and broadcasters, towards having the whole question of the law relating to homosexuality re-examined. Though Cornford's 'Principle of Unripe Time' was invoked by R. A. Butler and later Henry Brooke, Home Secretaries in governments afraid of electoral repercussions, the Wolfenden Committee was appointed in 1954 and its Report of 1957 was widely discussed. But it was left to Lord Arran in the

House of Lords and to Humphry Berkeley, and after him Leo Abse, in a private member's bill in the House of Commons in 1967, to undo the Labouchere Amendment to the Criminal Law Amendment Act of 1885, which penalised homosexual acts between consenting adults in private. All this produced in Britain a freer climate of talk and opinion, paralleled in some other countries,[1] until now we find ourselves accustomed to open advertisement of meetings and rallies of homosexuals, something unthinkable only a few years ago.

But there had always been one class of persons, relatively small but important as an élite, on whose attention the subject of homosexuality was inescapably thrust—those who were brought up on the study of the Greek and Roman classics and ancient history. There was much deprecation of this dark shadow on the idealised world of antiquity. Those debates in Parliament showed how ill-informed were some current ideas about ancient attitudes towards it; and indeed you would find little about it in many standard works of reference. So I should like to try to elucidate what is by no means a pellucid phenomenon.

In the world presented to us by the Homeric *Iliad* homosexuality is not a feature. The friendship of Achilles and Patroclus, though deeply passionate, is not overtly homosexual.[2] When the ambassadors leave

---

[1] The Kinsey Report of 1948 was a catalyst in the United States.

[2] After Patroclus' death Achilles' favourite was Antilochus, son of Nestor. Other legendary pairs of devoted friends were Theseus and Pirithoüs, Orestes and Pylades, and in history Alexander and Hephaestion.

them at the end of Book 9, they retire to bed, each with a woman concubine, in opposite corners of Achilles' hut. It is only in later ages, as in Aeschylus' lost play *The Myrmidons*, that their relationship is assumed to be sexual. Again Prince Ganymede, son of Tros, because of his beauty, had been carried off to heaven by the gods, we are told, to be Zeus's cupbearer. But it was left for later, pederastic poets to cite the Most High as a precedent for their own amours. It is true that in Greek mythology there are plenty of stories of the love of male gods for mortal males; but we cannot tell whether or not these antedate the Dark Age that followed the fall of Troy in the twelfth century BC. Nor is homosexuality found in the world of the *Odyssey*. When Telemachus visits Nestor in Book 3, his host arranges that he shall have his only unmarried son to sleep beside him in the colonnade; but it would be rash to deduce anything more than courteous companionship from that.

The poet—or two poets—whom we call Homer, shaping these two epics substantially as we have them in the second half of the eighth century BC (it would seem), was careful to preserve intact the bygone heroic age with which they dealt. But in the nearly contemporary Hesiod also, the earliest personal poet, there is no mention of homosexuality either, though he dealt with his own age; and it was the love-affairs of heroines that dominated the lost Hesiodic Corpus. Yet in the seventh and sixth centuries it was ubiquitous in the Hellenic world, as in the personal poetry of Stesichorus and Archilochus, Sappho and Alcaeus, Ibycus and Anacreon, and finally Pindar, now mostly known to us only in fragments and from hearsay.

Homosexuality itself is bound to exist everywhere

and in all ages, inasmuch as we may assume that the genetic make-up that conditions the sexuality of human individuals has always varied in such a way that hardly anyone will be 100 per cent male or female, and some will be very much of a mixture. The Kinsey Report used for assessment a spectrum graded 1–6. Active homosexuality will occur sporadically in societies where positive taboos against it are not too strong. But it will only be widespread where it is overt and given cultural encouragement. How did such a situation come about in seventh-century Greece?

A long-standing explanation has been that it was introduced in the Dark Age by the Dorians, the last of the races that invaded the Greek world. There was some colour for this. For instance, such practices were especially attributed to their favourite god, Apollo, and their favourite hero, Heracles. They appear to be more institutionalised in Dorian states such as Crete and Sparta. However, they also flourished in some non-Dorian states, being particularly uninhibited in Elis and Boeotia, while homosexual scenes on vase-paintings were a speciality of Athens. The theory is at best not proven. In any case the Dorian invasions are a rather problematical subject.

We should think of these practices as evincing bisexuality rather than homosexuality, in that they could coexist with family life, which remained the organisational basis of society. Surprisingly, to our way of thinking, we rarely hear of their being considered likely to disturb normal sexual relations between man and wife, perhaps because the marital relationship was not generally passionate. It is interesting to learn, however, that in an earlier version of Euripides' *Hippolytus* than the one we have Phaedra used her husband Theseus' relationship with Pirithous to justify her making passionate overtures to her stepson.[3] For various reasons our evidence about Greek attitudes to homosexuality is confusing. Items may refer to widely separated ages (five centuries divide Plutarch from Plato), or different states, or different social classes. Also there was in later times a flourishing industry in *chroniques scandaleuses*, many no doubt apocryphal, whose products we find garnered in such works as the 13th Book of Athenaeus' *Deipnosophists*. And, on the other hand, whitewashers may have been at work, including perhaps Xenophon and Plutarch.

Nor is it easy to discern why and how this Greek idiosyncrasy took hold. The seclusion of women may seem an obvious reason, but it cannot be a complete one. In Ionia, the coastal area of Asia Minor, where they were particularly secluded, it never became an institution, whereas in neighbouring Aeolia, where they were not, it inspired the poetry of Alcaeus (not to mention Sappho). It flourished in Athens, where women were somewhat secluded, but equally in Dorian Sparta and Crete, where they were not. Several ancient authorities thought that tyrants suppressed it because it was capable of inspiring passions reckless enough to overthrow them, as the lovers Harmodius and Aristogiton overthrew the Pisitratids at Athens.

[3] When Polemo (later head of the Academy from 313 to 270) was young his wife brought a suit against him for maltreatment because of his addiction to pederasty. Orpheus was alleged to have turned to pederasty after his loss of Eurydice because after her no woman could please him.

But it is hard to generalise. One is driven back to the opinion of Plato, persistent in antiquity, that it was ultimately bound up with the development of athletics and gymnastics. These were practised naked, produced beautiful bodies, and in some states at least gave occasion for young men to mix with boys. There is a steady increase during the fifth and fourth centuries in the proportion of statues of boy victors at Olympia, as recorded by Pausanias. 'I melt', wrote the Boeotian Pindar, 'when I see the fresh young limbs of boys.' Their development in some states was part of a policy of manly training for defence which also involved mess life (*syssitia*) and the spirit of loyal comradeship it bred. The old Homeric warfare of princes with their retainers fighting in the cause of some other prince has given place to the line of disciplined infantry fighting for its country. The important thing to realise is that the love of a young man for an adolescent was regarded as the best possible means to education. He would long to mould him to an ideal and to shine in his eyes, while the boy would long to emulate his lover and win his approval. Either would be ashamed to let the other down in a crisis, and this was a keen spur to valour. Such relationships, far from seeming effeminate, were considered the height of manliness.[4] A small, wedge-shaped stone found on the Acropolis at Athens bears a fifth-century inscription, 'Lysitheos declares that he loves Mikion more than all the boys of the city because he is brave.'

At Sparta such pederasty was the basis of education,

[4] Cf. the homosexual chivalry that flourished from about AD 1200 in parts of Japan, among the Knights Templar, and in Albania down to this century.

both technical and moral, an education regulated through family, society, state and religion, just like an arranged marriage. At the age of twelve an upper-class 'Spartiate' boy became eligible for a lover. A youth of similar class would sue for him, and if approved, take over the father's role. It was considered unseemly for tangible inducements to be offered, and we are told that a desirable boy could be fined for accepting a rich suitor in preference to a better but poorer one (though it is hard to conceive how the assessment could be made). An able-bodied young Spartiate who did not take on a boy, and an eligible Spartiate boy who acquired no lover, could be penalised. The law held the lover responsible for the boy's development, and the boy's reputation, good or bad, reflected on him. The lover was called the 'inspirer' (*eispnelos*), and the boy his 'hearer' (*aïtes*). The day on which the compact was made was a great occasion for the families and friends too. The lover gave his boy a suit of armour, and began to initiate him into the practice of arms. In the circumstances beauty could not be the sole, or even the prime, reason for choice; courage and character were no less sought on both sides. Yet the relationship seems to have been romantic. The object of the whole arrangement clearly was to perpetuate a tradition of martial excellence in an aristocratic caste, and to quicken it with emotional sentiment.

Similar institutions prevailed in the Cretan aristocracy. There was an elaborate ritual of courtship by simulated rape, analogous to the marriage ritual of Sparta. Giving three or four days' notice, a young man would intimate his intention to abduct a boy. Then, if both families approved, he would carry him off, after a token resistance, to his man's quarters (*andreion*), and thence for a sort of honeymoon to a country house, where he also entertained his friends to feasting and hunting. After two months he brought him back. If the boy complained that he had been subjected to violence, reparation had to be made and the affair was broken off; but if he said he had been well treated, he received from his lover (*philetor*) a suit of armour and a bull to sacrifice to Zeus at a feast for those who had accompanied them. He became his lover's comrade-in-arms (*parastatheis*). Boys thus favoured were called 'the honourable' (*kleinos*). They had special places in choirs and gymnasia, and wore for life a distinctive garment.

Most famous of such élite corps was the Sacred Company of Thebes, consisting of 150 pairs of lovers. Founded in 378, it was invincible until annihilated forty years later, after heroic resistance, at Chaeronea. Beside the body of the noble Epamindonas on the field of Mantinea was found that of his loved Asopichus, and they were buried together.

Both Spartans and Cretans are said to have sacrificed before battle to the god Eros. In general, Eros represented erotic sentiment, love, whereas his mother Aphrodite represented the physical manifestations of sex, lust.[5] Though both were concerned with either the heterosexual or the homosexual, Aphrodite was naturally more concerned with the former, Eros with the latter. Eros was represented in art as a dignified and handsome youth; it was only in the Hellenistic Age

[5] 'The enjoyment of Aphrodite without Eros can be bought for a drachma' (Plutarch). Eros had no recognised cult in Plato's time: 'his true temple is the soul of men' (Xenophon).

that he came to be a rascally, puckish boy, even a little child, often in multiplicate, presaging the Roman cupids and their descendants, the Renaissance *putti*. [6]

At Athens homosexual love had no connection with military chivalry, yet in the sixth and fifth centuries it was all-pervasive. There the custom (*nomos*) was, as Plato makes Pausanias explain in the *Symposium*, much more complex than in other states, which were either completely permissive, as in the case of Elis and Boeotia, or prohibitive, as in the case of many Ionian cities under the rule or influence of Persia. There were laws, attributed to the wise Solon, forbidding slaves either to take part in gymnastics or to have sexual intercourse (presumably without their master's permission) with a freeborn boy, partly no doubt to prevent their becoming 'uppity' through gymnastic or sexual prowess, partly to prevent their infecting free boys with the debased ethos of slaves. [7] This might suggest tacit approval of such affairs when between citizens. Yet schools and gymnasia were put out of bounds to men in the prime of life, that is, under forty or so, at times when the boys were there and in the hours of darkness. No one under forty could train a boys' choir. Any citizen who engaged in sexual activity for money was disqualified for life, as unclean, from the privileges of citizenship. Each tribe had an official

[6] We first hear of these as appearing in Aëtion's picture of the marriage of Alexander to Roxana (327 BC), playing with his armour; cf. the *putti* in Botticelli's *Mars and Venus* in the National Gallery.

[7] We learn from Demosthenes that there were laws, with the possibility of summary execution, against rape. These extended to the rape of slaves; in that case, he emphasises, it was the nature of the act, not the person, that the State regarded.

called *sophronistes*, guardian of the morals of its young.
Moreover, individual fathers appointed for their son an
escort (*paedagogos*) whose duties included seeing that
no lover communicated with him. Any boy who was
having an affair was liable to be teased by his contem-
poraries. Lysias in Plato's *Phaedrus* has to reckon that a
boy may hesitate to yield to a seducer out of respect for
the *nomos* or conventions of society.

All this points to general hostility among ordinary
people to pederastic practices. But the complexity
referred to by Plato's Pausanias arose from the differences and illogicalities involved in what actually went
on. The *nomos* encouraged the lover to pursue and the
boy to flee. (Professor Sir Kenneth Dover, one of the
few scholars who has freely discussed such matters,
compares the modern situation in which many parents
encourage their sons to make love but are horrified if
their daughters do so.)

At all events, by the fifth century those precautions
had ceased to operate. Socrates, whose insatiable love
of boys is frankly emphasised by his disciples Plato and
Xenophon, who were yet at pains to clear him of any
charge of corrupting the young, spent much of his time
hanging round schools and gymnasia.[8] We have also
the direct testimony of countless Athenian vases,
which from the third quarter of the sixth century to the
third quarter of the fifth are often inscribed 'so-and-so
is beautiful', or simply 'the boy is beautiful'. Boys'
names occur nearly twenty times as often as girls'.

[8] Xenophon depicts him as experiencing a *frisson* when accidentally rubbing shoulders with the beautiful Critobulus over a book
at school.

They generally suggest aristocratic birth. Some recur often, and in more than one painter—obviously those guaranteed to make a vase a best-seller. Some are known to us from history. Nine are familiar from the Socratic circle. Many vases depict scenes from the gymnasium or wrestling-school, and in some physical eroticism is overt. Handsome youths are also prominent in the sculptures of the Parthenon frieze. There was, as we saw, something like a cult of youthful male beauty. Sophocles may stand as an example of the spirit of the times at Athens. He was exceptionally beautiful; and as a boy he was chosen to lead the victory procession after the Battle of Salamis, naked, anointed and playing his lyre. He became proverbial for his love of beautiful boys, and several of his lost plays had homosexual themes.[9] Such were the people who set the tone of society.

Let me interject here a few remarks about the nature of such relationships. They were generally, in the classical period at least, entered upon by youths or young men with boys who had attained puberty, roughly aged twelve to eighteen. We must remember that, because of military commitments, men married rather late. Homosexual affairs between adults are less often in evidence. Adult pathics who used make-up and walked in a mincing way (*kinaidoi*) no doubt found partners;

[9] In his *Colchides* Zeus was enflamed by Ganymede. One of his satyr plays was called *The Lovers of Achilles*. Euripides' *Chrysippus* represented the curse on Thebes as beginning with the rape of that son of Pelops, by Oedipus' father Laïus. He was reputed to have written this play for his beloved Agathon. It was probably a seventh century epic by Pisander that made Laïus the introducer of homosexual practices to Greece.

121

but they were objects of opprobrium to the majority—comic poets, for instance, could expect their audience to laugh or shudder at them. In pederastic affairs it
was assumed that one party was older than the other
and took the initiative: we do not often encounter boy
Lolitas.[10] Indeed the vase paintings suggest that the boy
is doing a favour to someone who has won his affection
rather than enjoying himself. The lover was usually a
young man, though not necessarily so: Pindar was
apparently already middle-aged when he fell in love
with Theoxenus of Tenedos. A defendant in Lysias
admits, 'I may have been rather silly about the youth
for my age, but I hope you will not think the worse of
me for that, since all men are liable to passions.' It
seems to have been taken for granted that boys and
young men would go through a homosexual stage
before settling down in marriage. It was not a matter of
inversion, or even perversion, but of an expected stage
in life.

Inevitably the question arises: were such relationships physical? Let us begin with the poet Sappho,
who flourished in Lesbos about 600 BC, since we
may briefly deal once for all with what later acquired
the name of lesbianism. She had a cultural circle of
young girls, as did some other women there whom she
names; but it seems to have been as unofficial as
Socrates' circle of boys later on. These circles may have
been the women's reaction to the prevailing craze for
male homosexuality. Some of the fragments of her

[10] The word *paederastia* denoted the love of an older male for a
boy, *kinaidia* (and other, slang terms) a disposition in a male to
invite buggery. There was no general term covering our own
'homosexuality'.

poems to her girls are as passionate as any love-poems could be. Three or four are capable, if no more, of a physical interpretation, and in one can be read almost for certain the word for the leather-covered phallus or dildo used by lesbians, *olisbos*. But we hear singularly little of lesbianism in the ancient world, as indeed in the modern, partly no doubt through feminine reticence, and partly through the smallness of the proportion of female to male writers. To Queen Victoria its very existence was unimaginable.

It is a surprise to find Solon, the Athenian lawgiver of the early sixth century who, as we saw, was credited with those stern precautionary laws, referring to pederasty in fragments of two poems in unmistakably physical terms and as though it were a normal stage in a young man's development. The Greek vocabulary for homosexual relations distinctly implies that *coitus per anum*, or at least *inter femora*, was the normal form, and many passages in literature have the same implication. Graffiti on rocks in the Dorian island of Thera (Santorin) dating from the sixth century or earlier leave no doubt about what went on there. No sharp distinction was drawn between buggery and other forms of erotic play, though *coitus per anum* may have been considered as equivalent to treating as a woman, by contrast with *coitus inter femora*; whereas in Britain almost down to modern times it was literally a matter of life and death, and the Wolfenden Report, with four dissentients, retained the differential, not for any rational reason, but because of 'long and weighty tradition' and the presumption of 'a stronger instinctive reaction' in normal people, plus the curious argument that what was called 'the extreme form' was worse because it most resembled the normal act. However, Greek vases indicate that normally a boy stood and was taken in front between the thighs without himself being sexually aroused.

With regard to the Cretan and Spartan couples, in theory at least, physical eroticism was forbidden. The pro-Spartan Xenophon and some later writers insisted that this prohibition was effective, however incredible it might seem to people in many permissive states. We must not be automatically cynical. Among the warlike Albanians of the nineteenth century there were similar pairs; and although love was expressed in passionate terms, anything physical that went beyond a kiss on the forehead was considered worthy only of disgusting Turks. Cicero accepted a compromise version, that at Sparta everything was permitted so long as a blanket separated the partners. (One is reminded of those mediaeval lovers who tantalised themselves by sleeping with a sword between them.) All one can say is that it would be surprising if the flesh did not sometimes prove too weak, and the scepticism of many ancient writers, from Plato to Plutarch, is understandable.

At Athens indeed there were male brothels, served by slaves who were hired out by their masters or kept by brothel-keepers, and there was a tax on male prostitutes, annually confirmed by the Council. Phaedo was reputed to have been a prisoner-of-war rescued by Socrates from a brothel. One of Lysias' speeches, *Against Simon*, involves a contract for the services of a boy. In Aristophanes' *Frogs* the mire of Hades awaits those who cheat boys of their contracted pay. These would probably be the freelances who called at houses or hung about at night in dark regions such as the Pnyx and Mount Lycabettus, selling themselves, if not for money, for presents or *la dolce vita*. It would naturally be hard to prove either that any physical act had occurred or that money had passed.

It would be a mistake, however, to suppose that (in Athens at least) homosexual practices were smiled upon by everyone, at any rate after the middle of the fifth century. Xenophon spoke of them as 'something of the greatest reproach among us'. Indeed the whole vocabulary of euphemisms for them is pejorative (apart from one common in literature, *charizesthai*, to grant one's favours), especially as regards adult pathics. It was these, and not the active partners, who were abused and derided. Aristophanes' plays abound in satire on pathics, notably on the poet Agathon in the *Thesmophoriazusae*, who was old enough to have won his first victory as a dramatist five years before. That he was voicing his own sentiments is shown by what he says *in propria persona* in the Parabasis of *The Wasps*. One explanation of the conflict of evidence may be that homosexual behaviour was more fashionable in aristocratic and highly cultured circles, among the people who bought elegant vases or read Plato, than in the population at large. Yet Aristophanes, even if we discount his being assigned a part in Plato's *Symposium*, probably moved in such circles. It is unsafe to suppose that because the audience was not shocked by jokes about homosexuality and because comic 'heroes' are represented as enjoying it such conduct would be approved in real life.

By far the most reliable evidence we have for normal opinion, at least in the fourth century, is the speech of

125

Aeschines against Timarchus (delivered in 346). If only we had Demosthenes' reply! Timarchus was supporting Demosthenes in prosecuting Aeschines for treason. Aeschines counter-attacked by accusing Timarchus of having in his youth, though a citizen, prostituted himself for money. From this speech we learn, among other things: what reactions could be expected from a jury of ordinary citizens, their probable distaste for the whole subject; the text of those old laws for the protection of boys, still nominally in force; how a citizen who was a pathic might behave; that Aeschines himself could afford to admit to the court that he had had homosexual affairs, and was still liable to experience such passions, and that he had written verse about them. He distinguishes between commercial sex (which he calls disgusting, ridiculous and effeminate) and love (*eros*), which he approves—not between the physical and the aphysical. Admitting that in the nature of things he could have no direct evidence, he reminds the jury that Rumour (Pheme) was a great deity to whom their forefathers had set up an altar. And so horrified were they by his mere innuendos of commercial sex that they condemned Timarchus. What shocked them was that a citizen should have demeaned himself to do what would not be disapproved in an immigrant: sell his favours for money. We must remember that there were plenty of foreigners living in Athens.

The heyday of the beautiful boys of Athens waned in the second half of the fifth century, as aristocratic social traditions were replaced by democratic. Not suddenly, of course; Socrates, as we saw, was still obsessed with them. But they ceased to be celebrated on vases, nor were scenes from the gymnasia and wrestling-schools any longer portrayed. With increased specialisation in athletics, tough professionals superseded graceful amateurs in Greece as a whole during the fourth century. It is true that Plato was writing in the first half of that century; and right down to the fourth century AD Sophists and rhetoricians were to continue the debate raised by his Pausanias in the *Symposium* as to whether homosexual was better than heterosexual love (and we have just seen that Aeschines could say about the former in 346). But in the so-called New Comedy of that century, a fair index of public taste, love-interest centres on courtesans, or on problems of married life; and love as part of marriage is central to the plots of such plays as Menander's *Arbitration* and *Ill-natured Man*.

Consider what Plato has to say about love. In his *Symposium* Phaedrus sets the balling rolling by asserting that there can be no greater benefit for a boy than to have a worthy lover, nor for a lover than to have a worthy object for his affection. He makes specific reference to courage in battle; but that love could also be conceived as inspiring non-military education had already been illustrated in the sixth century by Theognis, the aristocratic poet of Megara, who addressed his lucubrations on life to a boy he loved named Cyrnus. In the next speech in the *Symposium* Pausanias distinguishes between the common Aphrodite *(Pandemos)* and the heavenly *(Ourania)*. Common love is inferior because it is directed at women as much as youths, and actually prefers its objects to be as unintelligent as possible; whereas heavenly love is exclusively male, and prefers boys beginning to show intelligence to mere children. Pausanias does not say that there should be no consummation in physical intercourse, but that on the part of the elder it should be primarily a love of the soul, of character rather than looks, and on the part of the younger a cautious and deliberate yielding motivated by desire for improvement. This speech was probably intended to represent the justification for pederasty that the better kind of Athenian gentleman of that time would give.

The culminating speech, that of Socrates, describes enlightenment he claims to have received long ago from a wise woman of Mantinea, Diotima. It gives the subject a new metaphysical dimension. Love of beauty first seen in an individual can and should broaden into love of all physical beauty; then lead to revaluing of moral and physical beauty, so that the loved one need not be good-looking at all if he excels in spiritual qualities; and thus by gradual process to the final achievement, the contemplation of divine and absolute beauty, which is identical with truth and goodness. That is Platonism.

But there is a concomitant theme. Love is a manifestation of the universal human desire to procreate, to perpetuate oneself. Those whose creative urge is physical have recourse to women and beget children. But in some the desire is for spiritual children, for begetting thoughts; and this can be achieved by intimate association with beauty embodied in a young friend. That is Socraticism; for we may fairly assume[11] that it was Socrates' idea that the old Greek sexual pederasty,

[11] It must be realised that all we know of Socrates' views on sex comes from Plato or Xenophon, but the two writers do here by and large corroborate each other.

portrayed at its best in Pausanias' speech, could be
transfigured by becoming a sublimation of sexual libido
into a common quest for truth and all other ultimate
goods which would elevate both lover and beloved. The
innovation lies in the belief that sexual intercourse takes
the steam out of this process. It is emphasised by the
scene that follows in the dialogue, when Alcibiades,
greatest of all Socrates' many passions, comes in drunk
and reveals to the company how once he tried to secure
for himself Socrates' sovereign educative help by making love to him, and how Socrates abstained all night
from taking advantage of this.

That this was indeed Socrates' attitude to physical
pederasty is borne out by another of his disciples,
Xenophon. In Xenophon's *Symposium* Socrates
praises love of the soul as against that of the body.[12] It
involves a self-restraint that is willing and pleasurable.
Affection is reciprocated because the boy recognises its
disinterestedness. His soul becomes the more lovable
the more it progresses in wisdom, and the two enjoy
caring for one another. These graces too are a gift from
Aphrodite, and they are lifelong; whereas physical love
is liable to be wasted on one whose soul is displeasing.
Bloom soon fades, feeding on beauty surfeits, and the
affection evaporates. Seduction is even worse than
rape, for it corrupts the soul as well as the body of the
seduced, who will concentrate, not on improving his
soul, but on exercising his charms. Besides, the boy,
unlikely to share keenly, as a woman does, in the
physical pleasure, may be disgusted, and come to find
the persistent beggar for favours a bore.

[12] Neither this nor Plato's *Symposium* prevented his being misrepresented as a practising homosexual in later times.

In the *Phaedrus* Plato represents the youth of that name as reading to Socrates a speech by the fashionable rhetorician Lysias which has excited him by its virtuosity, on the thesis that it is better for a boy to grant his favours to a non-lover than to a lover. Socrates, in rivalry, treats Phaedrus to a far more eloquent speech, describing the disadvantages of yielding to a passionate love, which is as the desire of the wolf for the lamb. But instead of going on to develop the other half of the thesis, on the advantages of yielding to a non-lover, Socrates suddenly disowns the speech he has made, as blasphemy against the god of love; and in a magnificently eloquent and imaginative recantation he praises passion as a divine madness. Love that is inspired by it can, if it transcends the physical, confer truly Olympian victories; and even if the couple prove unable to resist the physical urge, at least their wings will have begun to sprout.

> These blessings [Socrates concludes], so great and so divine, the friendship of a lover will confer on you. But the desire of the non-lover, which is alloyed with mortal prudence and calculating principles of conduct, will beget in the soul of the recipient the narrowness which the common people praise as virtue. It will cause the soul to be a wanderer upon the earth for nine thousand years, and a fool below the earth at the last.

Such is the rationale of Platonic love.[13]

[13] Though Plato (at *Republic* V 468) lets Socrates playfully suggest that the bravest soldiers should be rewarded by being allowed to kiss the most attractive boys, he did not approve of physical intercourse with boys.

A modern, especially perhaps an English educationalist might ask: 'Would not a boy like Charmides, whom Plato so vividly describes as the cynosure of every eye, be spoiled by the attentions of older lovers?' One may certainly feel that the behaviour of the adult Alcibiades, who had had so many admirers in his youth, was that of a spoilt child. Plato was aware of the danger, and makes Socrates in the *Lysis* reproach Hippothales for the poems he writes which make his boy vain and proud. He himself, on the contrary, hopes to make his beloved Lysis more circumspect and modest, by talking to him in a way that makes him realise and confess his ignorance. One has to recognise that many of those who have proved the best educators in our schools and colleges have been Socratic in temperament, such as William Johnson (Cory), the poet of *Ionica,* at Eton in the last century. Plato believed that the spirit needed a stimulus that was ultimately sexual in order to exercise its educative function. On the other hand one has to think of the effect on the boys who cannot inspire any emotional reaction, surely a majority today if not also in antiquity. Might they not suffer from inferiority complex and neglect if this were the chief basis of education? And does this not matter?

As to the psychological effect upon boys of homosexual experience, one must realise that, whereas some modern boys, seduced by an elder male, may find the experience traumatic, Greek boys took such experience, first passive then active, in their stride, and usually seem to have turned out largely or completely heterosexual in their adult practice.

I now come to Plato's one-time disciple, Aristotle. His

promise in the *Politics* to discuss elsewhere whether homosexual institutions are good or bad is not fulfilled in any extant work; and the treatises on sexual matters that we know him to have written are lost. But from casual remarks we can perceive his realistic attitude.

Whereas Plato talked chiefly of passionate love *(eros)*, Aristotle talked of friendship *(philia)*. To him friendship had three possible aims, education, advantage and pleasure. In love-affairs, assumed to be between young man and boy, the former sought pleasure, the pleasure of the eye, the latter advantage in the form of attentions and gifts. The lover was disappointed at the boy's lack of the kind of response he hoped for: he himself aimed at pleasure, and fed on beauty, both of them transient things; whereas true *philia* was something deep and durable. (Here Aristotle is, as often, too cut and dried in his distinctions in the psychological sphere.) Aristotle had a distaste for physical homosexual practices, as Plato and Xenophon had. They seemed to him worthy only of barbarians like the Celts—a notable reversal of traditional Greek feeling. And unlike Plato (though not Xenophon) he saw *eros* as the basis of the family, which was anterior to the state and essential to it.

In one important respect, however, Aristotle's disapproval was more discriminating than Plato's. In the *Republic* Plato said that there should be a law forbidding a lover to do anything to his boyfriend that a father would not do to his son. Late in life, when he came to compose the *Laws*, he had lost even the degree of tolerance he had shown in the *Phaedrus* for passionate lovers who found themselves unable to resist physical temptation. Abandoning for once his admiration for Sparta and Crete, he repeatedly expresses condemnation of homosexuality. In so doing he calls it 'unnatural', using an argument he would not have admitted in another context—that it is not found in the animal world.[14] But anything that occurs in nature is natural. It is rather odd that Plato should have come to take this line, considering that in the *Symposium* he had shown himself capable of devising an imaginative myth (put into the mouth of Aristophanes) of how it had come about, by the agency of Zeus himself, that varieties of sexual make-up exist in human beings, including that of both male and female homosexuals.

So it was that the emotive, question-begging phrase 'unnatural vice' early took root in the Western world, to the detriment of rational approaches to the subject. In the Lords debate in 1957 Archbishop Fisher said roundly, 'Nature makes both heterosexuals and homosexuals alike—there is no doubt about that. We are told with authority that, in varied proportions, both tendencies are present in every one of us.' The Wolfenden Committee decided to eschew the expression 'unnatural'; and in the subsequent debates it was used only by a few speakers such as Sir Cyril Black and Mr William Shepherd (who took the Committee to task for their decision) and, of course, Field-Marshal Montgomery.

Aristotle's approach, on the contrary, is that of an honest scientist. He recognises that predominately male embryos can acquire female characteristics, and *vice versa*, in the womb. In the *Physiognomica* some successor of his gives a detailed list of the characteristics of the pathic; and in the *Problemata* another speculates

[14] Actually it does occur among animals, e.g. hyenas, rarely however unless the sexes are separated.

on what maladjustment of the body causes him to have the physical desires he has. He himself distinguishes between congenital and conditioned homosexuality—in modern parlance, between inverts and perverts—a distinction which the Wolfenden Commitee was to find 'not very useful' for purposes of social legislation. In the *Ethics* he says that some people are homosexual by nature and others by habit, such as those who have been conditioned by being abused from boyhood. And he adds the all-important judgment, that no one could call those in whom nature was the cause profligate (*akrateis*, lacking in self-control), not those who are, through habituation, in what must be considered a diseased condition. Elsewhere in the *Ethics* he says:

> The appetite for food is natural since everyone who is without it craves for food or drink . . . and for love also (as Homer says), if he is young and lusty. But not everyone craves for this or that kind of nourishment or love, not for the same things. Hence such craving appears to be our very own. Yet it has of course something natural about it. (W. D. Ross).

He is here allowing that the abnormal can in a sense by called 'natural'. In the Loeb edition, where Aristotle uses the word *atopos*, 'abnormal', of some pleasure, Rackham misleadingly translates it as 'unnatural'.

In the Hellenistic Age philosophers continued to theorise, and rhetoricians to debate, about *eros*. We know the titles of ten works on the subject emanating from Plato's *Academy* and Aristotle's *Lyceum*. The headship of the Academy is said to have passed from lover to beloved for three generations, though this may have been rather a case of what we should call favourite pupils. Diogenes the Cynic, though his cult of shamelessness might have led him to approve of homosexual practices, seems from various anecdotes to have been hostile to homosexuals. This might have been in accordance with his principle that we must live according to nature which was inherited by the Stoics, if he shared Plato's interpretation of the word 'natural'.

The Stoic School, founded about 300 BC by Zeno of Citium, at first took a Platonic view of *eros* and its place in education, Zeno, reputed to have been homosexual in his own personal inclinations, laid it down that 'the wise man will love young people who show by their beauty a disposition to virtue . . . the bloom of youth is the flower of virtue'. But such talk was nebulous, not to say cant. As Cicero bluntly put it: 'Why does no one fall in love with a plain boy or a handsome old man?' And in fact the Stoics settled down to the view that all passion was bad. Here they parted company with Plato and approached their rivals, the Epicureans. These considered that *eros*, so far from being a divine dispensation, did you no good. You were lucky if it did you no harm. Sexual appetite was something to be satisfied, like hunger, in the readiest way, without sentiment. Sentiment was reserved for friendship, the most valuable thing in life.

In art and literature love was the great theme of the Hellenistic Age, the age of individualism. It could be either heterosexual or homosexual, as in Theocritus and the epigrams of the Anthology. But here tradition often overlay personal experience: we miss the direct evidence for real life that the fourth-century Attic

135

Orators had supplied. Meanwhile, the Hellenistic world was gradually being transformed into the Roman Empire.

In the early Republic the Romans' attitude to homosexuality was that of most non-Greeks; it was a Greek idiosyncrasy which they despised. They considered that gymnasium life had made the Greeks effeminate and undermined their military efficiency—the opposite of the old Spartan and Theban view; and the first great Roman poet, Ennius, said 'stripping among citizens is the origin of vice'. At first the law took cognisance only of rape, save that (as still with us) there were special prohibitions for soldiers on service, in the interests of military discipline. But in the second century BC, when captured Greece captivated its rude conqueror, there was an increase in homosexual practices; and at some time a *Lex Scantinia* was passed against them. This law was naturally hard to enforce, though it came in useful for trumping up charges in the law courts. As at Athens, it seems to have been adult pathics who continued in such ways *(exoleti)* that incurred most opprobrium. Respectable Romans always deplored them, the philhellene Scipio Aemilianus as much as the antihellene Cato, Cicero and Seneca alike. Julius Caesar felt that he had been indelibly smeared by Catullus' imputations. The Julian laws of Augustus prescribed the death penalty for sexual relations with free-born men and boys.

The qualification 'free-born' here highlights the fundamental difference between the attitude of Athenians and Romans, of Solon and Augustus, on this matter. Whereas Solon had forbidden slaves to partake in

homosexual practices, at Rome it was *only* slaves and
other non-citizens who could legitimately be used for
them; and they could be used without restraint. There
was something sacred about the person of a Roman
citizen. The Elder Seneca quotes from a speech a suc-
cinct sentence:

> Compliance is a stain in the free-born, a necessity in
> the slave, a duty in the freedman.

Trimalchio, the freedman in Petronius' novel, owed his
wealth to a master for whom he had served fourteen
years in the pleasure department *(ad delicias)*. 'Nothing
is disgraceful that the master orders', is his retrospec-
tive comment. Horace's remark, Epicurean in spirit,
that any sensible man requiring relief will have recourse
to the nearest slave boy or girl available (though made
in a satire deliberately aping a tradition and not to be
taken as necessarily indicative of what he would do
himself), reveals what was taken for granted in some
circles at least of society.

High prices were paid for beautiful slaves by private
owners. Some kept *paedagogia*, regular establishments
of beautiful boys, both home-reared and purchased, to
play the Ganymede for the delectation of guests as well
as master. The agriculturalist Columella warned
masters against selecting their farm foremen from
among slaves who had been used for such purposes.
There were also male brothels at Rome; and the male
prostitutes, *pueri meritorii,* had their own festival (on
April 24) as attested not only by Cicero but by fragments of a calendar that have survived. Romans may
have been attracted also, unlike most Greeks, by boys
under the age of puberty: Domitian stipulated by edict

that no boy should be prostituted under the age of
seven.

As for literature, at Rome experience was even more
overlaid with literary tradition, so that in the matter of
homosexuality we cannot tell what the poets themselves did, only that audiences were familiar with the
idea and at least tolerant of it.

Catullus addresses a cycle of poems to a boy he calls
Juventius; but he also protests elewhere that, while a
poet should himself be chaste, there is no need for his
verses to be so. Ovid specifically says that he is immune
from the love of boys because he dislikes any form of
intercourse where both partners do not achieve
orgasm, which is interesting as showing that to him
(unlike most Greeks of the classical period) pederasty
meant affairs with boys under the age of puberty.
Propertius hardly mentions the subject. Horace and
Tibullus show more interest, but not enough for us to
draw conclusions about their personal tastes and conduct, though Horace's description at the end of the first
ode in Book IV of the dreams he has about the
boy Ligurinus has a vividness that might suggest
experience.

The case of Virgil is different. He seems more involved.
The commentator Donatus says: 'Tradition has it that
he was inclined to desire for boys; but right-minded
people *(boni)* have thought that he loved them as
Socrates loved Alcibiades and Plato his boys.' With this
surmise I would agree, even disregarding such gossip as
that he pertinaciously refused Varius' offer to share his
mistress with him.

Virgil is not, in his major poems, a personal poet; but there is one short personal poem in the *Catalepton*, No. 5, which nearly all critics accept as his. In it he says goodbye to his associates at Rome when, as a young man, he is setting out for Naples and the Epicurean circle of Siro. Among these he includes *formosi,* which in Greek would be *Paides Kaloi,* beautiful boys, and particularly his 'chiefest love' (*cura curarum*), Sextus Sabinus. But even in the major poems we can, I think, discern an inclination. In the Second Eclogue Corydon's love is a boy, Alexis. One has to ask why, considering that the poem is a literary *tour de force* largely composed of motifs from heterosexual poems by Theocritus. I think that Virgil's own predilections are the most probable explanation. And in the *Aeneid,* though Dido is effective, if sometimes too rhetorical, as a tragic queen in the literary tradition of Medea, I feel it is with those young men killed in the flower of their youth while fighting in Italy, such as Lausus and Pallas, that the poet is really involved; and particularly with Nisus and Euryalus, a pair of lovers just like those of the Theban Sacred Company:

his amor unus erat pariterque in bella ruebant.
('These were united in love and charged together into battle.' 9. 178–83; cf 5, 295–6.)

Euryalus forma insignis viridique iuventa,
Nisus amore pio pueri.
('Euryalus outstanding in beauty and freshness of youth, Nisus in devoted love for the boy.')

It was *amor pius,* we are told, that bound the elder to the younger. If this implies that their love was sublimated, not physical, it is quite exceptional in Roman ideas; but not improbable in Virgil, nicknamed *Parthenias*, 'the virginal', whose well-attested shyness seems to have included something like a horror of sexuality.

Under the Empire homosexual practices continued to spread. It is clear from Lucian that, by the second century at least, the Scantinian Law was a dead letter. Sometimes a youth would set up house with a man as his *'frater'*, doing the shopping and housekeeping. As for the more sleazy types, the triangle between the three males who are the chief characters in Petronius' novel must have been recognisable as reflecting real life. But gossip was also active about some of the Emperors, about Tiberius (perhaps on scanty evidence), Caligula, Nero, Galba, Otho, and (as the final extreme) the openly pathic Elagabalus. Eunuchs—an Asiatic, not a Greek institution—were introduced and became the rage in some circles of society. Nero espoused Sporus, with all the honours generally accorded to an empress.

The most interesting case is that of Hadrian, a great philhellene. While touring in Asia Minor he fell in love with a beautiful Bithynian youth, Antinoüs, who became his constant company for nine years. I have already mentioned Antinoüs' effect on sculpture. When he was drowned on an expedition up the Nile (in AD 130), the Emperor's grief pervaded the Empire. He was deified, and identified with Mercury, Apollo, Dionysus, or Osiris. A newly-discovered star was claimed to be his soul. He became a subject for passion plays; and games were founded in his memory. This at least is evidence of passionate love, much more reminiscent of the affairs of sixth- and fifth-century Athens than the mere exploitation of slaves, which we must unfortunately take to be more typical of Roman homosexuality.

The Emperor Antoninus Pius was the first to introduce punishment for intercourse with an unwilling slave. Alexander Severus thought of prohibiting male prostitution, but abandoned the idea for fear of riots. Philip the Arab actually did prohibit it; but there was no great change, it would seem, until the coming of the Christian emperors.

The attitude of Christianity was influenced by its Jewish inheritance. The Law of Moses had explicitly condemned sexual acts between males. The fate of Sodom was there as an example; and St Paul, with his reservations on sexuality, had added his denunciations. Indeed to strict Christians, as in the ideal city of Plato's *Laws*, all sexual intercourse outside wedlock was a sin. Constantine revived Augustus' penalty of death by the sword for homosexual acts; and this was confirmed in 538, and again twenty years later, by Justinian, who denounced them as devil-inspired and a cause of pestilence, famine and earthquakes.

From then until our time in Christendom sodomy has been what the Law has called 'that abominable crime not to be named among Christian people'. Hence the wording of Housman's poem, which he never ventured to publish, evoked by the trial of Oscar Wilde:

> *Oh, they're sending him to prison for the colour of his hair . . .*
> *The nameless and abominable colour of his hair.*

The *Code Napoléon* made a breakthrough by not distinguishing in its prohibitions between heterosexual and homosexual acts, and Italy followed suit in 1889. But English and Scottish Law remained among the most severely discriminatory. What was achieved by the agitation leading to the Wolfenden Report of 1957 and the subsequent Sexual Offences Act of 1967 was, besides legal reform, a ventilation of the whole matter, leading first to a more rational and then to a more compassionate approach, and to a social climate which had made it possible for me to write as I have done.